THE
SCOTLAND
RUGBY
MISCELLANY

THE
SCOTLAND
RUGBY
MISCELLANY

BY RICHARD BATH

VSP

Vision Sports Publishing
2 Coombe Gardens,
London, SW20 0QU

www.visionsp.co.uk

Published by
Vision Sports Publishing 2007

ISBN-10: 1-905326-24-6
ISBN-13: 978-1-905326-24-2

Printed and bound in the UK by Cromwell Press

Typeset by Palimpsest Book Production Limited,
Grangemouth, Stirlingshire

A CIP catalogue record for this book is
available from the British Library

Mixed Sources
Product group from well-managed
forests and other controlled sources
www.fsc.org Cert no. TT-COC-2082
© 1996 Forest Stewardship Council

Vision Sports Publishing are
proud that this book is made
from paper certified by the
Forest Stewardship Council

By Gavin Hastings

I'm delighted to write the foreword to this book, which is full of facts, records and stories about Scottish rugby. I'm sure that fans of all ages, even those like me who have always been more interested in playing the game than reading about it, will find it stuffed with anecdotes and detail which will help bring the history of the game in our country to life.

From the time that I first picked up a rugby ball as a 10 year old at George Watson's College in Edinburgh, to the time I won the last of my 61 caps, against New Zealand at the 1995 World Cup, Scottish rugby has dominated my life. Even after my retirement I have remained intimately involved in the game – and I have loved just about every minute of it.

Inevitably, when I think about the history of Scottish rugby, I think about the matches I saw or played in. There are perhaps three moments that stick in my mind from my many years as a Scotland supporter and player, and they're probably not the ones you'd expect.

The first is watching from the stand as a nine-year-old in 1971 when Scotland played Wales in one of the most amazing games of all time. Wales were in their pomp back then, with all the great players like Barry John and Gareth Edwards, Merv the Swerve and J.P.R. Williams, but Scotland gave as good as they got in a see-sawing game that had the crowd on the edge of their seats. It was a game that got a fitting finale when John Taylor converted Gerald Davies' sublime last-minute try from the touchline to finally win the match. It was, they said, "the greatest conversion since St Paul". Who could resist the game after an afternoon like that? I was hooked.

The second moment that I really cherish is winning my first cap in 1986 at Murrayfield, and running out onto that pitch with five other new caps, including my brother Scott and Finlay Calder and David Sole. It's difficult to explain how exciting it was, but suffice it to say that I felt ten feet tall. I'd gone from playing in front of a couple of thousand people at Myreside to running out in front of 60,000 of my countrymen at the greatest stadium in Scotland.

Whether it's all the old photos of past players, the rolls of honour all over Murrayfield, or just being in those changing rooms deep in the bowels of the old stadium, it really brought home to me what it meant to play for Scotland, to be part of a story that started long before I was born and will keep going long after I'm no longer around. I was just intensely proud, and desperate to do my bit.

That day was a remarkable learning experience for me. Our captain Colin Deans took the time to come around each of the new caps on the morning of the First Test and there I was sitting watching television in the hotel room. I was sharing with John Rutherford, who was winning his millionth cap by then, but he was in the bathroom so nervous that it was all he could do to avoid being sick. Colin spoke to me about what it meant to play for your country, impressed upon me what an honour it was, and pointed to Rud as an example – even after all those years he was still so desperately worried about letting his country down that it hurt. He needn't have worried as we went on to win by 18–17.

But it wasn't just the game that sent shivers down my spine, it was the occasion and the legends who surrounded me. I'd grown up watching the big characters in the Scottish game – men like Andy Irvine, Jim Renwick, Ally McHarg and Mike Biggar – play here and then all of a sudden here I was, tackling Serge Blanco and then, after the game, going down to the Mitre pub in my kilt and dickie bow to knock down two or three pints with the other players before the Presidents Reception. I knew I was following in the footsteps of past legends and it was a great feeling.

During a long playing career I was lucky enough to be part of several amazing teams. In 1984 I was part of a victorious Cambridge University team in the Varsity Match, I played for a winning Lions side in Australia in 1989 and captained the Lions that narrowly lost the series to the All Blacks in 1993, with both squads having a sizeable Scottish contingent.

Even those achievements were eclipsed by the times I enjoyed with Scotland. I was the first Scot to have the honour of captaining Scotland Schoolboys to victory over our English counterparts, but it was the team that came together at the end of the 1980s and the beginning of the 1990s that really brings back the memories. The legendary 1990 team, for instance, was one which came together perhaps purely by luck but which was as good as any to have played for Scotland in the modern era. We won a Grand Slam then and reached the semi-final of the 1991 World Cup. Even at the end of my career there were some great times, such as when I scored the winning try against France in 1995 as we finally won in Paris after literally decades of trying.

Yet the final episode that is particularly dear to me is going out to New Zealand for the first World Cup in 1987 and then staying out for four months after the tournament ended. That opened my eyes, made me realise that although I thought I was a good player in my own back yard I still had much to learn. I played for Auckland University with four World Cup winning All Blacks in David Kirk, Grant Fox, Sean Fitzpatrick and John Drake. They were as committed in training as we were in matches; it taught me something which I brought back with me from New Zealand and tried to pass on to all the players I came into contact with.

This book reminds us that Scotland were there right at the beginning of the rugby story, and that we've played a huge part in the game's development and history. We should embrace that sense of history and use it to push ourselves so that we retain our place at the top table of the world game. If this book helps remind aspiring young players of how good we can be if we give it our all, then for that alone it is well worth reading.

Gavin Hastings

— ACKNOWLEDGEMENTS —

I'd like to thank a number of people who have helped immeasurably in the production of this book. First among those is Nick Oswald, the statistician and historian whose help and attention to detail made the compilation of this book more of a joy than a chore. As ever, any mistakes are mine and mine alone.

I'd also like to thank the SRU's indefatigable press officer Graham Law, Norman Mair, Mark Entwistle, Gavin Willacy and Gregor Townsend, who all fielded my occasionally bizarre enquiries with unfailing good humour. Ditto Vision Sports Publishing's Jim Drewett and copy editor Clive Batty, both of whom displayed a commendably tolerant approach to my laissez-faire attitude to deadlines.

Finally, I'd like to thank my family – Bea, Ollie, Ailsa and Lochie – for putting up with yet more absences and grumbling from the study.

Richard Bath

Author's note: Unless otherwise stated, all statistics refer to events up to the end of the 2007 Six Nations.

— SCOTLAND'S RUGBY ROOTS —

The game of rugby arrived in Scotland with two young brothers, Francis and Alexander Crombie, who moved to Edinburgh from Durham in 1854. The younger of the two, Francis, was enrolled at Edinburgh Academy. Neither had played rugby, but knew the rules, which they passed on. Although too old to be a pupil, Alexander helped set up the Edinburgh Academical Football Club under a rule that said relatives of pupils could be members of the club, and from 1858–64 he was its first captain.

Shortly afterwards and completely coincidentally, rugby arrived at the Royal High School when an English boy named Hamilton arrived at the school with a written set of the first 'Rules of Rugby Football'. The game quickly took root in the RHS.

Contrary to accepted wisdom, the first match between two schools occurred on February 13th 1858 when the Royal High School played Merchiston (many people believe that because Edinburgh Academicals' annual match against Merchiston is the longest-standing continuous fixture in world rugby, that it must be the oldest).

— ALL THE FOES —

Scotland's record against the other Test-playing nations*:

	P	W	D	L	Abandoned
England	124	41	17	66	0
Ireland	120	61	5	53	1
Wales	112	48	3	61	0
France	80	34	3	43	0
New Zealand	25	0	2	23	0
Australia#	25	7	0	18	0
South Africa	18	4	0	14	0
Italy	12	8	0	4	0
Romania	10	8	0	2	0
Argentina	6	1	0	5	0
Samoa ^	6	5	1	0	0
Fiji	4	3	0	1	0
Japan	3	3	0	0	0
USA	3	3	0	0	0
Canada	2	1	0	1	0
Tonga	2	2	0	0	0
Zimbabwe	2	2	0	0	0
Ivory Coast	1	1	0	0	0

Spain	1	1	0	0	0
Uruguay	1	1	0	0	0
SRU President's XV	1	1	0	0	0
Total	558	235	31	291	1

\# Includes match v NSW Waratahs in 1927

^ Formerly Western Samoa

* Up to the end of the 2007 Six Nations

— THE FIRST INTERNATIONAL: THE CHALLENGE —

At the Kennington Oval in March 1870, England's soccer team beat a 'Scotland' team featuring London-based players with varying degrees of Scottishness (one said he had a fondness for whisky, another that he came north each year for the Glorious Twelfth). When the secretary of the FA, C.W. Alcock, tried to rearrange a return match, he wrote to several Scottish papers inviting them to nominate players, but received only one reply – hardly surprising given that there were only four soccer clubs in Scotland at that time (Queen's Park, Thistle, Hamilton and Airdrie).

Sensing another humiliating defeat by the English, the captains of the five Scottish rugby clubs sent the following letter-cum-challenge to *Bell's Life* and *The Scotsman*. Published on 8th December 1870, it led directly to the first international at Raeburn Place, Edinburgh.

Sir, There is a general feeling among Scotch football players that the football power of the old country was not properly represented in the late so-called International Football Match. Not that we think the play of the gentlemen who represented Scotland otherwise than very good – for that it was so is amply proven by the stout resistance they offered to their opponents and by the fact that they were only beaten by one goal – but that we consider the Association rules, in accordance with which the late game was played, not such as to bring together the best team Scotland could turn out. Almost all the leading clubs play by the Rugby code, and have no opportunity of practising the Association game even if willing to do so. We therefore feel that a match played in accordance with any rules other than those in general use in Scotland, as was the case in the last match, is not one that would meet with support generally from her players. For our satisfaction, therefore, and with a view of testing what Scotland can really do against an English team, we, as representing the football interests of Scotland hereby challenge any team selected from the whole of England to play us on a match, twenty-a-side, Rugby rules, either in Edinburgh or Glasgow on any day during the present season that might be found suitable to the English players. Let this count as the return to the match played in London on 19th November, or, if preferred, let it be a separate match. If it be entered into we can promise England a hearty welcome and a first-rate match. Any communication addressed to any one of us will be attended to.

We are, etc

A.H. Robertson, West of Scotland FC
F.J. Moncrieff, Edinburgh Academical FC
J. Hall Blyth, Merchistonian FC
J.W. Arthur, Glasgow Academical FC
J.H. Oatts, St Salvador FC, St Andrews

— SHORT OF THE LINE —

On their first visit to Twickenham in 1911 the Scottish players were unable to find the entrance and had to walk through the adjoining allotments to get into the ground.

But once they'd found their way in Scotland put up a good fight and were leading when centre G. Cunningham broke two tackles and sped off towards the English posts for what looked a certain try. However, just as he looked to be heading over the line, a despairing tackler managed to get a hand onto his shorts, ripping them off him. Rather than take the three strides to the line, the mortified Cunningham simply sat down as the 25,000 spectators roared with laughter.

That comic caper seemed to turn the tide and England ran out unexpected 13–8 winners. Scotland would only win four Calcutta Cup contests at Twickenham before the turn of the century, while Cunningham would never play for Scotland again.

— FASTEST TRY . . . EVER! —

The fastest try scored for Scotland was by John Leslie on his international debut at Murrayfield in 1999, when he scored a try against Wales after just nine seconds. The try came when stand-off Duncan Hodge switched direction, kicking off to the left and away from the two sets of forwards. As Welsh full back Shane Howarth waited to field the ball, Leslie rose and plucked it out of his hands, going over for the fastest international try ever scored.

— THE FIRST INTERNATIONAL: THE TEAMS —

The Scottish challenge of 8th December 1870 (see *The First International: The Challenge*, page 2) was ignored by C.W. Alcock, the secretary of the English FA, but was spotted by B.H. Burns, a Scot who played at Blackheath and doubled as the club's secretary. Burns accepted the challenge and two committees were set up to select the two sides. Scotland had two trial matches, one in Glasgow and one in Edinburgh, while England picked 12 players from London and four each from the two northern strongholds of Liverpool and Manchester.

The two sides met at Raeburn Place, in front of 4,000 spectators, on 27th March 1871 and lined up as follows:

Scotland: W.D. Brown (Glasgow Academical), T. Chalmers (Glasgow Academical), A. Clunies-Ross (St Andrews University), T.R. Marshall (Edinburgh Academicals), J.W. Arthur (Glasgow Academical), W. Cross (Glasgow Academical), A. Buchanan (Royal HSFP), A.G. Colville (Merchistonians and Blackheath), D. Drew (Glasgow Academical), J.F. Finlay (Edinburgh Academicals), J. Forsyth (Edinburgh University), R.W. Irvine (Edinburgh Academicals), W.J.C. Lyall (Edinburgh Academicals), J.L.H. Macfarlane (Edinburgh University), J.A.W. Mein (Edinburgh Academicals), F.J. Moncrieff (Edinburgh Academicals, captain), R. Munro (St Andrews University), G. Ritchie (Merchistonians), A.H. Robertson (West of Scotland), J.S. Thomson (Glasgow Academical).

England: A. Lyon (Liverpool), A.G. Guillemard (West Kent), R.R. Osborne (Manchester), W. MacLaren (Manchester), F. Tobin (Liverpool), J.E. Bentley (Gipsies), J.F. Green (West Kent), R.H. Birkett (Clapham Rovers), B.H. Burns (Blackheath), J.H. Clayton (Liverpool), C.A. Crompton (Blackheath), A. Davenport (Ravensourt Park), J.M. Dugdale (Ravenscourt Park), A.S. Gibson (Manchester), A. St G. Hamersley (Marlborough Nomads), J.H. Luscombe (Gipsies), C.W. Sherrard (Blackheath), F. Stokes (Blackheath, captain), D.P. Turner (Richmond), H.J.C. Turner (Manchester).

Umpires: H.H. Almond (Scotland), A. Ward (England)

Scorers: Scotland: Tries: Buchanan, Cross. Conversion: Cross. England: Try: Birkett.

— SCOTLAND'S GREATEST GAMES 1 —

Scotland 1 goal, 1 try, England 1 try
Raeburn Place
27th March 1871

A lot has been written about the genesis of the first 20-a-side game of international rugby, but less of what actually happened at Raeburn Place. It was a perfect spring day in Stockbridge, and over 4,000 spectators paid 1/- (5p) to watch as Scotland captain F.J. Moncrieff kicked off from the Inverleith end shortly after 3pm with a light breeze at his back. The chosen pitch was a narrow one to thwart England's fast, inventive backs, so the game was dominated by the forwards. The match was scoreless at half-time, but only thanks to the intervention of the English forward Osborne, who ran full tilt at James Finlay as he was about to ground the ball, almost knocking both men out in the process.

There had been other close shaves before the interval. At one stage Scotland carried the ball over the line but the English claimed to have touched it down, while both Turner and McLaren narrowly missed kicks at goal. However, the home side's territorial dominance began to pay dividends in the second half, and after Richie was denied a pushover try which he insisted was good even when on his deathbed, Angus Buchanan was driven over for the first international score, converted into a goal by Cross (crucially because it was goals that counted, not tries). The English argued vociferously that the try should not stand, but with so many assailing umpire H.H. Almond, he gave the score (see *Umpire Punishes Noisy England*, page 37).

England fought back, mainly through J.F. Green, a speedy back who made several mazy runs through the Scottish defences. But when he was tackled so hard by Chalmers that he had to leave the pitch and never played rugby again, Scotland were in the ascendant. Ironically, 19-man England, despite visibly tiring in the face of an onslaught by their fitter opponents, scored a try shortly afterwards through Birkett, but Stokes failed to convert. Scotland rounded the game off with a try 90 seconds before the end when, with their forwards running riot, J.W. Arthur knocked on from a line-out and the ball looped over the English defenders, with the quick-thinking Cross picking it up for Scotland's second try. Although the English again protested, Almond pointed out that a knock-forward was only illegal if it was deliberate, and the try stood, giving Scotland the emphatic win that their superior play and fitness merited.

— KIWIS CASH IN —

During the first major incoming tour, when Dave Gallaher's All Black 'Originals' of 1905 played at Murrayfield, the tourists asked for a guaranteed match fee of £400 to cover their touring costs. The SFU balked at this, offering instead to let the Kiwis have the gate receipts after expenses had been deducted. The New Zealanders had little choice but to accept and were delighted when a capacity crowd at Inverleith provided gate receipts of almost £2,000 and a payment to the tourists of £1,700 – a sum that was more than four times what they had originally asked for. It wasn't a mistake the Union would ever make again.

To add insult to injury, Scotland were beaten 12–7, a loss partly attributed to the late withdrawal of Dr A.N. Fell, the New Zealander who was attending Edinburgh University and who was one of Scotland's key players, but who refused to play against his countrymen.

— MOST CAPPED XV BY POSITION —

15. Gavin Hastings, 61 caps
14. Tony Stanger, 47 caps (total of 52 caps, including five at centre)
13. Scott Hastings, 60 caps (total of 65 caps, including five at full back/wing)
12. Jim Renwick, 51 caps (total of 52 caps, including one at wing)
11. Kenny Logan, 68 caps (total of 70 caps, including two at full back)
10. Craig Chalmers*, 55 caps (total of 60 caps, including five at centre)
 9. Bryan Redpath, 60 caps
 1. Tom Smith, 61 caps
 2. Gordon Bulloch, 75 caps
 3. Paul Burnell, 52 caps
 4. Scott Murray, 84 caps
 5. Stuart Grimes, 71 caps
 6. John Jeffrey**, 40 caps
 7. Finlay Calder, 34 caps
 8. Simon Taylor, 45 caps (total of 53 caps, including eight as a flanker)

*Gregor Townsend won more caps than Chalmers but only 50 of them were at stand-off, with 32 as a centre and a further six appearances off the bench – total of 82 caps.
**Jason White has won 57 caps, but approximately 20 have been won as a second-row

— SCOTLAND LEGENDS XV: MARK MORRISON —

A rough, tough gentleman farmer, Morrison was one of Scotland's finest early players and the first genuine star of the game north of the border. A no-nonsense utility forward who played for the Royal High School FPs in Edinburgh, he combined pace, strength and a prodigious work-rate with a hard-nosed attitude which made him a feared opponent.

The figures alone do not encapsulate a man who was larger than life, but they do go some way to explaining why he was such a giant of the Scottish game. Morrison captained his country 15 times during a 23-cap career that lasted from 1896 to 1904, a record that stood until Arthur Smith's era almost 70 years later.

He captained Scotland to Triple Crowns in 1901 and 1903 and remains the only skipper to have won three Calcutta Cups. No other captain of Scotland has come close to equalling the bald statistics of his time at the helm: nine wins, two Triple Crowns and three Championships in five years.

From his early schooldays Morrison was a renowned heavy-hitting and fearless tackler, and hailing from the rugby hotbed of the Royal High School the Scotland selectors were soon aware of his prowess. Like many other of the game's early greats – men such as Ninian Finlay, Willie Neilson, Charles 'Hippo' Reid and Robert 'Bulldog' Irvine – he was capped out of school, and made his debut against Wales in 1896 aged just 18.

Despite the Scots' 6–0 loss in Cardiff he was an immediate sensation and three years later he was to captain his country for the first time against Wales, this time at Murrayfield where there was a discernible change in the performance of the Scotland side. From a hit-and-miss outfit, they became remarkably consistent, losing just four of the 15 games in which he was skipper – three of them in the year Scotland suffered their first whitewash, 1902.

Morrison's air of quiet authority was noted by the Lions selectors, who chose him to lead the side to South Africa in 1903, where he found the standard of play had improved beyond anything the touring British players had expected. Morrison was devastated to become the first Lions captain to lose a series when he returned with two draws and a loss to his name after a series of provincial losses (out of 19 games, the tourists won just 11).

Yet no-one reproached Morrison. In fact, he was lauded by opponents for his robust play: "a real rough house of a player and a great leader," was how Jimmy Sinclair, the famous Springbok forward who doubled as a cricket international, described the Scot after the final, losing Test.

Morrison didn't completely disappear from rugby when he retired aged 29, serving as the president of the Scottish Rugby Union between 1934 and 1935 before his death in 1945. He also lives on as one of the handful of rugby inductees in the Scottish Sports Hall of Fame, and through his great-great-grandson Iain, who won 15 caps on the openside for Scotland in the mid-1990s.

Mark Morrison stats
Caps: 23 (1896–1904)
Position: Utility forward
Club: Royal HSFP

— SCOTLAND'S TOP SCORERS —

Most points

	Tests	Tries	Cons	Pens	DGs	Total
Gavin Hastings (1986–95)	61	17	86	140	0	667
Chris Paterson (1999–07)	74	21	65	106	2	559
Andy Irvine (1972–82)	51	10	25	61	0	273
Kenny Logan (1992–03)	70	13	34	29	0	220
Peter Dods (1983–91)	23	2	26	50	0	210

Most tries

	Tries	Tests
Ian Smith (1924–32)	24	32
Tony Stanger (1989–98)	24	52
Chris Paterson (1999–07)	21	74
Gavin Hastings (1986–95)	17	61
Alan Tait (1987–99)	17	27
Gregor Townsend (1993–03)	17	82

— LIGHTS ON, THEN OFF —

The first floodlit match in Scotland took place on 24th February 1879 in Hawick when the Green Machine took on Melrose, whom they defeated by a goal to nil. There was a crowd of at least 5,000 and gate receipts of £63, although these would have been higher had there been more than one man on the gate and no holes in the perimeter fence. The power for the floodlights came from two steam engines, which were turned off at the final whistle, causing chaos as spectators skidded through the heavy snow in the darkness.

— RULE DISPUTE SPARKS BOYCOTT —

Scotland's objections to a match-winning try that gave England the championship in 1884 led directly to the formation of the International Rugby Football Board (IRFB).

More than 8,000 spectators had travelled to Blackheath to watch England and Scotland, both of whom were unbeaten, play in the title decider. The match turned on a fumble followed by a knock-back by Scots forward Charles Berry, which England picked up to put Richard Kindersley in for a try.

Under Scottish rules a knock-back was illegal, whereas in England it was completely acceptable, however the English players argued that the Scots shouldn't benefit from their own mistake. The problem was that the Scots refused to accept the result, a dispute which led to the Scots denying the right of the RFU to be the sole arbiter of fact, which in turn led to the 1885 fixture being cancelled.

It was only with the formation of the IRFB in 1886 that there was a resolution, although the English refused to sanction the establishment of the IRFB and pulled out of the Championship for two years between 1888 and 1890 as a result of the row.

— SCOTLAND'S FIRST TRIPLE CROWN —

Scotland's first Triple Crown came when they defeated England by three goals to one at the Richmond Athletic Ground on 7th March 1891. The Scotland scores were a dropped goal by P.R.A. Clauss after ten minutes and then second half tries from J.E. Orr and young back Gordon Neilson (one of three brothers to have played for Scotland), both of them converted by McGregor.

— WHOSE SIDE ARE YOU ON? —

James Marsh remains the only player to have turned out for two different sides in the International Championship. Marsh was a former Edinburgh Institute pupil who qualified from Edinburgh University and played for Scotland against Wales and Ireland in 1889. He then moved to Manchester and played a single match for England in 1892 against Ireland.

— SCOTS HERE, THERE AND EVERYWHERE —

Scots were to the fore in the opening Test of the 1903 Lions tour to South Africa, providing both captains and the referee.

The Springbok skipper, Alex Frew, was from Kilmarnock and had won a Triple Crown playing for Scotland under Mark Morrison. He had then emigrated to the Transvaal, as had Saxon McEwan, another Scotland forward who had won 16 caps between 1984 and 1900. The Lions captain was Scotland breakaway and skipper Mark Morrison, who had been first capped as a teenager and became Scotland captain in 1899. Morrison held onto the post until 1905, during which time he led Scotland to Triple Crowns in 1901 and 1903.

The referee was Bill Donaldson, a former Loretto and Oxford Blue who won six caps for Scotland in the 1890s and was the first man to score at Scotland's new Inverleith home.

The Test ended in a 10–10 draw, with Frew scoring one of the two Springbok tries. The Second Test was also drawn, with the Springboks winning the third – a taste of things to come as they didn't lose a home series for 55 years.

— UNLICENSED —

Three Scotland international backs – Rowan Shepherd, Derek Stark and Gregor Townsend – got together and bought a bar in Edinburgh's Grassmarket, calling it the 'Three-quarters Bar'. It was a popular haunt on international rugby days . . . until it emerged that the building did not have a license.

— LONG DAY OUT —

The longest regular fixture in Scotland occurred when Newton Stewart and Orkney were in the same league, a round journey of some 480 miles from Galloway to Aberdeen, followed by a seven-hour ferry ride each way between Aberdeen and Kirkwall. The round trip took 26 hours – even before the rugby and post-match entertainment was added on.

— OVAL AND ROUND BALL INTERNATIONAL —

The only Scot ever to play both soccer and rugby for Scotland was Henry Renny-Tailyour of the Royal Engineers. He won a solitary cap at rugby, in the loss to England at the Oval in 1872, and also a single cap at football, which he also won against England.

Renny-Tailyour won his only football cap in bizarre circumstances in 1873 when England hosted Scotland at the Oval in a match now recognised as the first official international soccer match. The fledgling Scottish FA could only afford to send down eight players, so three more had to be found. As a prominent Scottish player with the Royal Engineers, then one of the strongest sides in England, Renny-Tailyour was an obvious choice. He didn't let them down: although Scotland lost 4–2, Renny-Tailyour scored the visitors' first goal, making him the first man to score a goal for Scotland.

The India-born striker was a regular at the Oval in those days, appearing in three FA Cup finals with the Royal Engineers, including the first one in 1872. That match ended in a 1–0 defeat for the Royal Engineers at the hands of Wanderers, but Renny-Tailyour was back in 1874, this time being beaten 2–0 by Oxford University. He finally got his winner's medal in 1875 when, after drawing 1–1 with the Old Etonians, he led the line for the Royal Engineers side which beat the old boys 3–0, with Renny-Tailyour scoring in both matches.

As well as being a rugby and soccer dual international, Renny-Tailyour was an accomplished athlete and a first-class cricketer who played 28 games for Kent. A middle order batsman and occasional bowler, he also played for Aberdeenshire and appeared for the Gentlemen against the Players, as well as turning out for the MCC, the South of England and a combined Kent and Gloucestershire XI.

A colonel in the army, he became Managing Director of Guinness after he retired from the army.

— BILL'S ADVISORY ROLE —

Scotland was the last of the major Test-playing nations to appoint a national coach, although the SRU insisted on calling him the "adviser to the captain". The first man to get the job in 1971 was Bill Dickinson, a forwards coach of huge talent who doubled up as a lecturer at Jordanhill College.

— DOMINANT SCOTS —

The unstoppable Scotland team of the 1920s

Scotland were the first team to win at Twickenham, beating England 17–9 in the 1926 Five Nations. After winning a Grand Slam the previous year, they finished equal top in 1926, only missing out on a second consecutive Grand Slam when they lost 3–0 to Ireland.

Indeed, so dominant were Scotland in the late 1920s that they topped the Five Nations in four of the five years between 1925 and 1929. In 1928, the only year in which they failed to top the table, they finished joint last.

— POLICING THE LINE —

Either Wales or Scotland won every International Championship between 1900 and 1909. When the two sides met in February 1906 in Cardiff, the chief constable wanted to be present and patrolled the touchline in his full dress uniform for the whole game.

Unfortunately, when former Lions skipper and Scotland legend 'Darkie' Bedell-Sivright dribbled over the Welsh line for what seemed like a certain try, the ball struck the chief constable and although it came back into Bedell-Sivright's arms, it was ruled a non-try, leading directly to a change in the laws that any fan in the home in-goal area should be considered "in play".

— ANYONE GOT A SPARE SHIRT? —

There are several famous tales of the parsimony of administrators in the amateur era, including Tony O'Reilly's famous after-dinner tale of his days as a student when he had lost his socks and couldn't afford a new pair before a game, only being 'lent' a pair when he lined up to take the field at Lansdowne Road wearing none at all.

Scotland's Jock Wemyss would sympathise with him. Wemyss, a prop who had represented his country before the First World War, was selected to play in Scotland's first match after the end of hostilities, on New Year's Day in 1920 in Paris. The former Gala man had, as was the custom in those days, come with his Edinburgh Wanderers socks and shorts and was sitting in the Parc des Princes expecting to be given a shirt. However, when the bag man came around with the shirts, he walked straight past Wemyss without giving him a jersey.

When Wemyss asked why he had been passed over he was told that he was given a shirt on his debut in 1914 and should have brought that. Despite arguing that he had given it to his opposite number after the game against Ireland six years earlier, the bag man wouldn't budge. It was only when he took his place in the line-up wearing no shirt that one was finally produced.

As a potscript, Wemyss had something in common with his opposing prop that day, Frenchman Marcel Lubin-Lebrere – both had lost an eye during the war. After sharing a drink or five at the post-match banquet, the two men became lifelong friends. It is not known whether Lubin-Lebrere followed Wemyss's habit of carrying around a spare, bloodshot, glass eye to match his remaining eye after a few beers too many.

— LINDSAY'S TRY RECORD —

Scotland's George Lindsay holds the record for the number of tries scored in an International Championship match. The London Scottish three-quarter scored five of Scotland's 12 tries as Wales were crushed by four goals and eight tries to nil in Edinburgh in February 1887. Lindsay had not at first been selected for the match, which was originally scheduled to be played on New Year's Day, but made the team for the rescheduled fixture.

— GOING TO EXTREMES —

Tallest player: Richard Metcalfe first capped against England in the famous 2000 Calcutta Cup win at Murrayfield, measured a shade over 7' 0" (2.13m) and is the tallest man to have played international rugby.

Shortest: Graeme Beveridge at 5' 6", won the first of his six caps against New Zealand in 2000. To the amusement of many spectators, Beveridge and Metcalfe appeared together in three Tests in 2000!

Heaviest: Richard Metcalfe weighed in at 20st (127kg).

Lightest: Quinty Paterson weighed in at 8st 12lbs (56.25kg) and was capped against England in 1876. He was regarded as a good club player but even in those days he was too light to play international rugby and was easily brushed aside when attempting to make tackles.

Fastest: Eric Liddell, Olympic Games 400 metres champion would have a strong claim to be the fastest Scotland player. He won seven caps (1922–23) making his debut at Stade Colombes against France and two years later he returned to the same stadium to win his Olympic title.

— FLOWER OF SCOTLAND —

Although an anthem of Scottish supporters following the British Lions in South Africa in 1974, the first time 'Flower of Scotland' was officially played as the anthem of the Scotland rugby team was before the Grand Slam showdown with England in 1990.

The tune was written in 1966 by Roy Williamson of folk band The Corries, and refers to the victory of the Scots, led by King Robert the Bruce, over the English King Edward II at the Battle of Bannockburn in 1314. It was adopted in large part because 'God Save the Queen' was being continually drowned out by the ferocious booing and whistling of some Scotland supporters.

— NATIONAL WINNER —

Rubstic, the horse which won the 1979 Grand National, was owned by former Scotland international John Douglas, the No. 8 who won 12 caps out of Stewart's College FP between 1961 and 1963.

— CALCUTTA CUP ORIGINS —

The Calcutta Football Club, which was to donate the eponymous cup which is now played for each year between England and Scotland, was formed in January 1873, just a month after the first overseas game of rugby took place between a XX representing England and a XX representing Scotland, Wales and Ireland. The match, which took place on Christmas Day 1872 in Calcutta, was such a success that a second was played a week later.

One of the club's leading lights was B.H. Burns, a Scot who had turned out for England in the first international. However, the club began to falter after four years, due partly to a lack of opponents. Regular opponents the 3rd Buffs left India in 1876, partly because of the searing climate but more so the cessation of the free bar that had made the Calcutta club a social hub. At this point Burns seconded club captain G.A. James Rothney's suggestion that the £60 of silver rupees left after the club was wound up should be melted down and used to produce a trophy of ornate Indian craftsmanship.

The Calcutta Cup trophy is 18 inches in height, with two snakes for handles and topped off with a small elephant. The first Calcutta Cup game was played in 1879 at Raeburn Place and resulted in a draw.

— FOUNDING MEMBERS —

The Scottish Rugby Union was formed in Glasgow in 1873. Its founder-member clubs were Edinburgh University, Glasgow University, St Andrews University, Edinburgh Academicals, Glasgow Academicals, the Royal High School, West of Scotland and the Merchistonians.

— MONKEY BUSINESS —

Scotland refused to play Wales in 1898 and 1899 because the WRU had paid for a house for skipper Arthur 'Monkey' Gould through a testimonial fund.

When the furore started in 1897 they were supported by Ireland, but stood alone until 1899. The SRU also refused to play the touring Wallabies of 1908–09, and were leading the charge when the French were kicked out of the Five Nations for nine years in 1931 due to the taint of professionalism.

— BEATING ENGLAND TIME AFTER TIME —

At the back end of the 19th century following the loss of England's finest players when the northern Rugby League split away, Scotland became used to beating England. Indeed, when they travelled to Fallowfield in Manchester in 1897 to contest the Calcutta Cup against an England side who had scored just three points in the previous four matches between the sides, they were so confident of winning that they didn't even bother bringing the cup south. England, though, went on to register a shock 12–3 victory in front of 15,000 amazed spectators.

It didn't last, however, and Scotland's longest winning streak in England spanned the end of the 19th and beginning of the 20th centuries. In the last match before moving to their new home in Twickenham, England lost their sixth successive match against the Scots in 1909, going down 18–8 after leading 8–3 at half-time.

— NO NUMBERS ON THEIR BACKS —

The Scots were the last international team to number players. When Scotland played England at Twickenham in 1924, King George V asked the president of the SRU, the notoriously conservative J. Aikman Smith, why the men in blue had no numbers on their back, he was informed in clipped tones that: "This is a rugby match, not a cattle market".

— HOMES FROM HOME —

Scotland have not always played their internationals in Edinburgh. In 1906, for instance, they inflicted the touring Springboks' first reversal in 16 matches, an emphatic 6–0 defeat, in front of 40,000 spectators at a packed Hampden Park. The Springboks didn't lose another Test in the British Isles until 1965.

— BROWN'S EYE ACCIDENT —

Prime minister Gordon Brown is known for his love of football and for selling programmes at his beloved Raith Rovers, but he lost his eye playing rugby while a pupil at Kirkcaldy High School.

— SCOTLAND LEGENDS XV: DAVID BEDELL-SIVRIGHT —

Bedell-Sivright: The hardest man ever to pull on the dark blue jersey?

It would be easy to characterise 'Darkie' Bedell-Sivright, as he was known in those pre-political correctness days on account of his swarthy complexion, as a meathead. After all, there is little doubt that he was one of the toughest – if not *the* hardest – man ever to pull on the dark blue jersey, and no account of his play is free of liberal sprinklings of words such as "robust", "ferocious" and even "disregardless".

A loose forward by inclination, Bedell-Sivright was feted the world over for the intensity with which he played the game and for the relish with which he sought physical confrontation. And it wasn't just rugby: if he wasn't fighting his brother in the streets he would be off honing the boxing skills which made him the Scottish heavyweight champion. He even thought at one stage of becoming a jackaroo in Australia, before deciding that it was a waste of an expensive education.

Bedell-Sivright is one of the biggest characters in the history of

Scottish rugby and there are no end of stories of his madcap antics. One concerns the time in Edinburgh when he had been out for a night on the sauce after winning an international and decided to take a nap across the trams tracks on Princes Street – no policeman brave enough to move him could be found. When he finally woke after an hour, the first thing he saw was a carthorse, which he proceeded to knock over with a well-aimed flying tackle.

For all that, Darkie was known primarily as the most talented forward of his generation, a man who could turn games by sheer force of will. He made his debut as a 20-year-old against Wales in 1900 under Mark Morrison and went on to become the only Scot to win three Triple Crowns (1901, 1903, 1907). He also distinguished himself when touring with the Lions under Morrison's captaincy in 1903, going on to captain the Lions tour to Australia and New Zealand in 1904 as the only Scot selected.

Bedell-Sivright proved to be an inspired and inspiring captain who led by example and brought the best out of his players in Australia, where they won every game, including the three Tests. Just how important he was to the side became obvious when he broke his leg in Christchurch on the New Zealand leg of the tour: the previously unbeaten tourists only won one of the remaining four games in New Zealand, losing the Test.

Not that he had to wait long to meet the Kiwis, who toured Britain the following year. Indeed, although Bedell-Sivright captained every side he played for, he only captained Scotland once, against Dave Gallaher's 'Originals' in 1905, a match Scotland lost 7–12.

An accomplished pianist with a passion for literature, on his return from Australia he surprised everyone by studying medicine at Edinburgh University. His friends were even more amazed when he graduated with a first. That, however, was to be the death of him. Signing up to serve in the First World War as a navy surgeon, he died in the Dardanelles in September 1915 of acute septicaemia which set in after a gnat bite became infected. He was just 34.

"He just played this game for all it and he were worth, utterly heedless of all else during the 40 minutes each way," wrote E.H.D. Sewell in his obituary. "Certainly one who will be remembered and spoken of as long as the game is played."

David Bedell-Sivright stats
Caps: 22 (1900–08)
Position: Utility forward
Clubs: Cambridge University, Fettesian-Lorretonian, West of Scotland, Edinburgh University

— A GOOD START AT MURRAYFIELD —

Scotland may have been faring badly against the Auld Enemy immediately after the First World War, but the men in blue celebrated the official opening of Murrayfield in 1925 by beating Wavell Wakefield's side 14–11, registering both their first win over England for 13 years and notching up their first Grand Slam in front of 80,000 spectators.

— OPENING VICTORIES —

Scotland beat each of the other Five Nations members on first meeting: defeating England at Raeburn Place in 1871, beating Wales by three goals to one at Raeburn Place in 1883, Ireland by six goals to nil at Belfast in 1877, and France 27–0 at Inverleith in January 1910. Only Italy, who beat Scotland in 2000, prevented a full hand of first meeting wins.

— NUMBER CHANGE —

The 15-man game was the result of a petition by the SRU in 1875, which was adopted during the next season. Up to that stage, there had been 20 men per team.

— SCOTTISH CONNECTIONS DOWN UNDER —

The Ranfurly Shield, the most prestigious trophy in New Zealand rugby since its inauguration in 1902, was presented to the New Zealand Rugby Football Union by Lord Ranfurly, the Governor General of the country and a Scot who hailed from Renfrewshire.

New Zealand was heavily settled by Scots and many of its names owe much to the home country. 'Dunedin' is Gaelic for 'Edinburgh', for example, while other main centres such as Hamilton and Invercargill owe their names to Scots exiles (as does Perth in Australia and Brisbane, named after an area near Largs).

— RECORD WINS —

Scotland 100 Japan 3, McDiarmid Park, 2004
Scotland 89 Ivory Coast 0, Rustenberg, 1995 Rugby World Cup

— CHALMERS' FULL HOUSE —

A good day at the office for Craig Chalmers!

Craig Chalmers was the first Scot to register a 'full house' (try, conversion, penalty and drop goal), the big day coming in the 32–12 defeat of Wales at Murrayfield in 1991.

Frenchman J.P. Lescaboura, the first player to drop a goal in all four Five Nations games, completed the feat at Murrayfield in 1984.

— OUT FOR THE COUNT —

Former Scotland captain and Lions flanker Rob Wainwright won a Blue for Cambridge at boxing. He only ever had one fight, which he won when he knocked out his Oxford University opponent.

— QUOTE UNQUOTE —

"Baby faced Brown is a real meanie!"
Headline in New Zealand paper in 1971 that announced **Gordon Brown's** arrival with the all-conquering Lions

"There's no doubt about it, he's a big b*****d."
Gavin Hastings on Jonah Lomu

"Wainwright, you're like a lighthouse in the desert – brilliant but f**king useless"
Jim Telfer to Rob Wainwright after he dropped the ball for a third time in a rucking practice

"Like women, different scrummaging machines can take time to get used to."
Ian McGeechan

"Sorry for missing that penalty kick. I don't know what went wrong – it was such an easy shot, I could kick myself."
"I shouldn't bother, you'd probably miss."
Conversation between **Gavin Hastings** and **David Sole** after the 1991 World Cup semi-final when Hastings had missed a penalty in front of the posts with minutes remaining and the score at 6–6. Rob Andrew then went on to score the drop goal which put England in the final.

"Grandmother or tails, sir?"
Referee to Princess Anne's son **Peter Phillips**, Gordonstoun School's captain, for his pre-match coin-toss preference

"Winterbottom's playing today. He expects a kicking. Dinnae disappoint him."
Jim Telfer to Derek Turnbull before the 1990 Grand Slam decider

"It's like being a drug addict. We're on the bottom rung and the only way to go is up."
Unfortunately, **Jim McLaren's** early prediction in the 2003 World Cup was proved wrong

"We feel it more than anyone else, but we do apologise."
Chris Paterson after Scotland were beaten 51–9 by France at the 2003 World Cup

"The French lifted up the Scottish kilts and found they had no balls."
Zinzan Brooke hits Scotland where it hurts after the 51–9 defeat by France in the 2003 World Cup

"We've been trying to build towards it, we're quite excited about it."
Ian McGeechan on Chris Paterson's switch to fly-half in the must-win 2003 World Cup game against Fiji – something he fought against for the first 40 caps of the Gala man's Test career

"We have become the laughing stock of the World Cup."
Scotland great **Scott Hastings** on the 2003 World Cup defeat by France

"That's the first time I've seen a try scored live and in slow motion."
Jim Renwick to Bruce Hay when the Boroughmuir full back scored his first try for Scotland

"One day you're a rooster, the next you're a feather duster."
Wallaby coach **Alan Jones** after Australia had beaten Roy Laidlaw's Grand Slam Scotland side 37–12 at Murrayfield, a defeat that came hot on the heels of a 28–22 defeat to Romania in Bucharest

"Flodden is at last revenged."
Reaction of **James Carmichael**, a master at Edinburgh Academy, when Scotland beat England in the first international at Raeburn Place in 1871. The battle of Flodden was fought in 1513.

"Scavengers."
England coach **Geoff Cooke** on Scotland

"We tend to think in our own little midden that we are good, and we are not."
Jim Telfer after the All Blacks second string beat the South 84–5 in 1993

"I like quick teams – not necessarily quick players but sides that overall are fast."
Ian McGeechan

"Now their status as one of the proudest rugby countries in the world is in tatters."
Findlay Calder after Scotland beat South Africa 21–6 in 2002

"Everybody knows that I have been pumping Martin Leslie for a couple of seasons now."
Murray Mexted

"It was tremendous, unbelievable, the sun is shining in my house."
Former Scotland and British Lions coach **Jim Telfer** from a rainy Galashiels as Scott Gibbs' try saw Wales beat England at Wembley in the last minute of the last game of the 1999 Six Nations to deny the men in white a Grand Slam.

— MAROON COLOUR CLASH —

When Stewartry started life in the sleepy town of Newton Stewart in Galloway, they wondered what colour their jerseys should be. They alighted on maroon because, "the only team which plays in maroon is Gala and we'll never find ourselves in the same league as them". That was back in 1922 when Gala were one of the most powerful clubs in Britain, let alone Scotland.

However, in 2007, Gala dropped into the third tier for the first time – where they found themselves playing against promoted Stewartry. How the mighty are fallen.

— ZUT ALORS! —

Scotland were the first of the home unions to be beaten by France, sustaining a 16–15 loss in Paris in January 1911. The win was all the more remarkable because France started the match a man short after one of their players was caught in traffic and only arrived midway through the first half.

— THE WINNER TAKES IT ALL —

The first winner-takes-all Five Nations match happened in 1913 when England and Scotland met in the Calcutta Cup at Twickenham. England won 3–0 courtesy of a try from naturalised Australian L.G. 'Bruno' Brown. The next such showdown was to be at Murrayfield, 77 years later, when the result was memorably reversed.

— REFFING CONTROVERSY —

Scotland refused to play France in 1914 due to what the SRU considered the excessive barracking of opposition officials and intimidation of referees by the French, particularly when England came from behind to win in Paris. It turned out to be a lost opportunity for one of the sides: both countries ended the Championship with no wins.

The issue was to raise its head again in 1927 when Scottish referee R.L. Scott needed police protection after a game in Paris between France and Ireland, and the SRU subsequently declined to send any of its referees to officiate in France.

— SCOTLAND AT THE WORLD CUP: 1987, AUSTRALIA AND NEW ZEALAND —

Scotland started the tournament fourth favourites after New Zealand, Australia and France, but had major injury concerns. John Beattie was out for the tournament, Scott Hastings was injured for the opening game against France, and Scots hopes took a further dent when John Rutherford landed awkwardly on a knee that had been injured in a minor tournament in Bermuda (that the SRU had ordered him not to attend!) and not only was his World Cup over, but so was his international career.

Although Scotland did well to draw 20–20 with the French thanks to an injury-time try from wing Matt Duncan after Serge Blanco had gone over for a sneaky try from a tap penalty while Scotland had been attending to the injured Duncan, France scored three tries to Scotland's two and went through as the top team in the group. The second-placed team were scheduled to meet eventual winners New Zealand, and a brave but out-gunned and injury-depleted Scotland were beaten 30–3 by David Kirk's men at Lancaster Park in Christchurch, with tries from flanker Alan Whetton and full back John Gallagher.

Pool matches:
Scotland 20 France 20
Scotland 60 Zimbabwe 21
Scotland 55 Romania 28

Quarter-final
Scotland 3 New Zealand 30

— TOWNSEND'S WONDER YEAR —

In 1999 Gregor Townsend became the first Scotland player to score a try in all four Five Nations games as Scotland won the final Five Nations trophy before Italy's arrival led to the tournament's enlargement. Although Scotland lost narrowly to England 24–21 at Twickenham, Townsend's tries helped them to an emphatic 36–22 win in Paris (all five Scottish tries came in the first half), a 30–13 thrashing of Ireland at Murrayfield and a 33–20 win over the Welsh in Edinburgh.

Townsend went on to be awarded the MBE that year for his services to sport. He is also Scotland's most-travelled player, having played at eight clubs in three continents: Gala, Warringah, Northampton, Brive, Castres, Montpellier, Natal Sharks and the Border Reivers. The only Scot in the modern game to come close is Scott Murray, who has turned out for Preston Lodge, Edinburgh Accies, Bedford, Saracens, Edinburgh and Montauban.

— HOT STUFF —

When the SRU installed undersoil heating at Murrayfield in 1961, it was the first Union to do so. The new system soon came in handy, sparing the pitch from the worst of the elements during the 'Great Freeze' of 1963.

— EARLY START, LATE FINISH —

When Wales entertained Scotland in the 1931 Five Nations in Cardiff, the capacity crowd turned up early on a beautiful spring day and the referee decided to allow play to start five minutes before the scheduled 3pm kick-off. With many legends of the game playing, it was a very open game and within three minutes Wales' Jack Morley had been put over in the corner to score.

Scotland's forwards dominated, though, and the pressure told with two tries by debutant flanker Donald Crichton-Miller before Watcyn Thomas, despite having a broken collar bone from an earlier tackle (there were no replacements in those days) levelled the scores with a try against the run of play. With the 40 minutes up, Wales launched one last attack, the Welsh backs probing deep into Scottish territory. Just as it seemed the attack had been snuffed out, a pass was flung at Harry Bowcott, the ball bouncing off his chest and spurting loose to wing Ronnie Boon – who hacked ahead and scored for a try that came so deep into stoppage time that it was after the scheduled finish.

— THE ULTIMATE SACRIFICE —

Perhaps because the Scots answered the call to arms more enthusiastically than any other part of Great Britain, the two world wars took a terrible toll on Scottish rugby, with 30 Scottish internationals perishing in the 1914–18 conflict and 15 between 1939–45, compared to 27 and 14 for England and a comparative handful for Wales and Ireland.

During the First World War the entire Watsonians first team took the plunge by joining up together in the 9th Royal Scots, the famous 'Dandy Ninth', losing three internationals in J. Pearson and E. Milroy, who both won 12 caps between 1909–13, and J.Y.M. Henderson who died a one-cap wonder after making his solitary appearance against England in 1911. Despite fierce losses, Watsonians won at Swansea in December 1919 to become the first non-Welsh side to win at St Helen's for over 20 years.

Yet the three clubs which lost most Scottish internationals in the First World War were based in England, with Cambridge University losing five caps and Oxford University four. Still, no rugby club in Britain was hit harder by the conflict than London Scottish. As with McRae's Battalion – the famous unit made up of Heart of Midlothian FC volunteers, of whom three-quarters were butchered on the Western Front on 1st July 1916 when they launched an assault on Contalmaison in the Somme – units of men recruited from sporting institutions were commonplace in the First World War and all four London Scottish units joined up together in August 1914, the first month of the conflict.

Of the 30 Scottish internationals killed between 1914–18, seven – including that giant of the game, former Lions and Scotland skipper David 'Darkie' Bedell-Sivright who perished of septicaemia at Gallipoli – came from London Scottish. In 1913 the club had four senior sides, numbering just over 200 playing members, all of whom joined the London Scottish Volunteers: only four of them returned to play unscathed. In those four years, 69 were killed, 50 were wounded and four were captured as prisoners of war. One of those who survived life in a German prisoner of war camp was Charles Usher, who went on to captain Scotland and win ten caps after the war.

— REGAL BAN —

In 1424, James I of Scotland issued an act banning the game of football. His successor James IV becomes the fourth Scottish king in the 15th century to ban the game when he passed another law in 1491.

— ERIC LIDDELL —

Eric Liddell: Scotland winger and Olympic champion

Immortalised in the film *Chariots of Fire*, Eric Liddell was an Olympic athlete who also won seven caps on the wing as an Edinburgh University student in 1922 and 1923, scoring an unforgettable try in the 1923 win in Cardiff before quitting the game prematurely to concentrate on athletics.

Such was his fame that even though he wouldn't win an Olympic gold medal in Paris until 1924, when he made his Scotland debut in a 3–3 draw in Paris in 1922, the gate receipts were 230,000 francs, then a record for any sporting event in France.

A devout Christian, Liddell died in a Japanese prisoner of war camp in 1945 after being captured while working in China as a missionary.

— FORWARD KICKING —

Scottish forwards who have dropped goals:

Charles Cathcart v England at The Oval on 5th February 1872
John Boswell v Ireland at Raeburn Place on 22nd February 1890
Matthew McEwan v Ireland in Belfast on 21st February 1891
John Boswell v England at Leeds on 4th March 1893
Peter Kinninmonth v Wales at Murrayfield on 3rd February 1951

In addition to these players, Charles Berry kicked a goal from a mark v Ireland on 19th February 1887. William Thomson also kicked a goal from a mark (on his debut) v Wales at Inverleith on 4th March 1899.

— NOT SO PROUD FATHER —

The father of Scottish internationals Dave and Bob Howie, who played for their country before and after the First World War, was a farmer who had no time for his sons' past-time. Indeed, although they played a total of 14 times for Scotland he never watched them once. His view was uncompromising: "Rugby and ferming will no' agree and I ken which'll put mair money in yer pooch."

— GRIM WEEK —

The worst week in the history of Scottish rugby? Although the 44–0 beating by the Springboks in 1951 could qualify, 10th-17th November 1993 is the most likely winner. That was the week in which the All Blacks beat Scotland's inter-provincial champions, the South of Scotland, 84–5 in their own backyard on a day that became known as 'Black Wednesday', and then beat the full Scotland side 51–5. As a postscript, Scotland romped home to the Wooden Spoon that season.

— THE SHIRT OFF HIS BACK —

The Barbarians' win over Swansea in 1958 was one of the roughest matches in the club's history. Scottish fly-half Gordon Waddell had his shirt ripped off his back three times, with the game held up each time while a replacement was sent for. He had the last laugh, though, scooting through the defence from halfway to put Welshman Roddy Evans over for the winning try.

— SCOTLAND LEGENDS XV: GAVIN HASTINGS —

Gavin Hasting: the greatest?

The greatest of all Scotland's rugby players, Gavin Hastings was a natural player and a natural captain. A big full back at 6ft 2in, he didn't have blistering pace but was a peerless footballer who could tackle hard, kick long and straight, take a high ball under pressure and be relied upon to take the right option at every opportunity. Everything came easily to the big Watsonians full back and there is little he failed to achieve in an international career spanning 12 seasons.

Hastings played for his country 61 times, won a Grand Slam and captained Scotland 20 times. He also captained the first Scottish

Schools side to win in England; captained Cambridge University to Varsity Match victory at Twickenham; captained the first Scotland team to win at the Parc des Princes; and captained the Lions in three of his six Tests.

Then there are the numbers and the records. Hastings scored a record 18 points on his debut alongside brother Scott as Scotland beat France 18–17; he ended his career with a record points total of 667; he remains Scotland's most capped full back; he holds the record for the most number of points scored in Lions Test matches at 66; the most points on Lions tours including provincial games (167); he holds the record for the most number of points scored in World Cup rugby with 198 in 11 games over three tournaments; and the highest number of points scored in a World Cup game with 44 against the Ivory Coast in 1995. Even his autobiography, *High Balls and Happy Hours*, has sold more than any other Scottish non-fiction book.

If Hastings had low points in his career, they were being beaten by England in the 1991 World Cup semi-final after missing a kick in front of the posts, being denied a series win with the Lions in New Zealand thanks to a refereeing error, being beaten by the last kick in the 1994 Calcutta Cup, and coming so close to beating New Zealand in 1990. But set against those setbacks are any number of true highs: scoring the try that beat France in 1995, a Lions series win in 1989, a Grand Slam in 1990 and being part of the World XV that beat the All Blacks.

Above all, though, Hastings' legacy is to be remembered as a Scot who could challenge to get into the all-time World XV. As Ian McGeechan once said: "Gavin is a big man in every sense of the word. His greatest asset was his ability to engender confidence in those around him and to lead by example when the opposition had to be taken on. In New Zealand they considered him simply the best."

Gavin Hastings stats
Caps: 61, (1986–1997)
Position: Fullback
Clubs: Cambridge University, Watsonians, London Scottish

— SOLE SCOT —

The only Scot who played in the Barbarians' famous 23–11 win over the All Blacks at Cardiff in 1973 was West of Scotland's Sandy Carmichael, who had had his cheekbone shattered by Canterbury prop Grizz Wyllie when touring with the Lions in 1971. Carmichael didn't feature in the build-up to Gareth Edwards' legendary try.

— SCOTLAND'S GREATEST GAMES 2 —

Scotland's 1990 Grand Slam heroes

Scotland 13 England 7
Murrayfield
17th March 1990

The 1990 Calcutta Cup win is unarguably the most famous match in Scottish rugby history, one of the few moments when a whole nation was transfixed by the sport. The reasons for that were many: on a wider level, anti-Englishness had been stirred by Margaret Thatcher's decision to trial the poll tax in Scotland; on a personal level, many of the Scots and English players had developed a healthy dislike of each other during the 1989 Lions tour, with players like Will Carling and Brian Moore becoming hate figures for Scottish rugby followers; and on a rugby level, this was a winner-takes-all Grand Slam decider.

Where Scotland had laboured to win their first three matches, the English had been in sublime form and didn't seem to have any inkling of what awaited them. Super-confident as they ambled around the Murrayfield pitch with their wives and girlfriends on the morning of the match, they soon found that the afternoon would be far harder than they had ever expected.

The first indication of Scotland's determination came before the kick-off when Scotland captain David Sole led his men out at a deliberately funereal pace in a manoeuvre that will be forever remembered as '*The Walk*'. Next came the new rugby anthem, with

'Flower of Scotland' sung officially before a Test match for the first time (and how it was belted out). All the time the crowd was in ferment, and as soon as the match kicked off the Scots were in about England, harrying them and refusing them the time and space to settle.

As Scotland pressed, so England made mistakes, two of which allowed Craig Chalmers to kick two penalties before a virtuoso try by England centre Jeremy Guscott, England's first at Murrayfield for a decade, brought it back to 6–4. But when Chalmers kicked another penalty just before half-time, a plainly disbelieving England went into the interval trailing 9–4.

The decisive moment of the match came seconds after the restart when scrum-half Gary Armstrong fed Gavin Hastings, who chipped ahead up the touchline for speeding wing Tony Stanger to let the ball bounce in front of him before plucking it out of the air to fall over for a try which sent the old stadium into raptures.

England's powerful forwards regrouped and for the remaining 40 minutes they battered the Scottish defences, their efforts becoming increasingly frenzied as the clock counted down. But try as they might, all they had to show for their efforts was a penalty from stand-off Rob Andrew. This was Scotland's third Grand Slam – but the fact that it was won by beating the Auld Enemy when least expected made it by far the most satisfying. England were stunned, but as the *Edinburgh Evening News* noted, the visitors "weren't playing a team, they were playing a whole nation".

— BORING, BORING WALES —

Scotland have the bad luck to have featured in what was arguably the most boring rugby match ever played. When Wales travelled north in 1963, they had just been beaten by England – a defeat for which they were roundly castigated.

Travelling to Murrayfield, a venue where Wales had lost four times in succession despite expecting to win comfortably each time, visiting captain Clive Rowlands decided to exploit his edge in the forwards and decreed that the ball would be kicked into touch at every opportunity and then driven. What followed was a match of a record 111 line-outs – most of them in the Scotland 25 – which was so stultifyingly, mind-numbingly dull that it produced a huge outcry. Wales won 6–0, not that many people were awake to care.

Ironically, the match did some good. So sustained was the hue and cry afterwards that kicking into touch on the full from outside the defensive 25 was prohibited and the off-side line was re-drawn.

— HASTINGS' RECORDS —

When Gavin Hastings' Scotland career came to an end he held the following records (some have since been beaten):

- Most points on his debut: 18 v France in 1986 through six penalties, which was also a record.
- Most caps: 61.
- Most Tests and points for the Lions: Six Tests over two tours and 167 points.
- Biggest individual points tally in a Test match: 44 v Ivory Coast at the 1991 World Cup.
- Most points scored for his country: 667 points.
- Most points scored by any player from any country in the World Cup: 198 in 11 games.

— CYRIL'S FRENCH LESSONS —

Many of the top administrators in world rugby have been Scottish-born. Among them was Cyril Rutherford, who led the French Union for much of the first half of the 20th century and was credited with overseeing their emergence into a genuine top-level rugby nation.

— ABANDONED MATCH —

Scotland versus Ireland in 1885 at North of Ireland's ground in Ormeau in Belfast is one of only two Test matches ever to have been abandoned after kick-off.

It was raining at kick-off, but a storm developed and after half an hour, with Scotland leading by a try, the referee called the two captains together and suggested a replay would be in order. That duly took place two weeks later at Inverleith, where Scotland dominated, winning by a goal and two tries.

The other match to be abandoned was during France's 1991 World Cup warm-up tour of North America, where thunder and lightning ensured the game in Colorado Springs had to be called off.

— KICKING FOR GLORY —

Two of the most famous last-gasp touchline conversions in the history of the game have happened in games in which Scotland have been playing. Both of them were kicked by back-row forwards, one giving Scotland a famous victory, the other consigning them to glorious defeat.

The so-called 'Greatest conversion since St Paul's' happened in 1971 during one of the most compelling and exciting Five Nations matches of all time and saw Scotland lose out in injury-time to a Wales side that went on to win their first Grand Slam for two decades. Trailing 18–14 with seconds left, the peerless wing Gerald Davies outflanked the Scotland defence for a truly brilliant try, but had to ground the ball in the right corner. Up stepped openside flanker John Taylor, who spent what seemed an age lining up the ball before kicking it straight through the uprights with his left foot. As the Welsh fans roared their approval, Taylor celebrated by leaping up and punching the air in a memorable victory salute.

The tables were turned weeks later, however, when Scotland skipper and No.8 Peter 'PC' Brown, did exactly the same to the English at Twickenham, kicking a late conversion that, in the words of Bill McLaren, "wobbled over the bar in an inebriated fashion" to give Scotland a 16–15 win. After years of drought against the Auld Enemy, Scotland became the first nation to beat England twice in a year when they beat England 26–6 at Murrayfield in the Centenary Challenge match to celebrate the first game of international rugby, which took place at Raeburn Place in 1871.

If those were two sublime, match-winning touchline kicks, undoubtedly the worst missed kick at the grand old stadium came in 1991 in the World Cup semi-final between Scotland and England, with the Auld Enemy on the rack and the Scots in full cry just a year after beating the men in white at the same venue to claim a Grand Slam. With the scores level deep into the second half and Gavin Hastings lining up a penalty straight in front of the posts, it seemed as if another famous win was just a kick away – before Hastings unaccountably sliced the ball wide. It was a mistake that hurt the normally unflappable Hastings like none before, as became clear in his tearful post-match apology after Rob Andrew went on to drop-kick England into their first World Cup final.

— WARTIME BOYCOTT —

No Scots took part in the wartime internationals. The SRU was alone among the Home Unions in boycotting them because the services teams included Rugby League players.

— SCOTLAND LEGENDS XV: IAN SMITH —

Born in Melbourne in 1903, brought up in New Zealand and educated at Winchester, Ian Smith remains the most prolific try-scorer ever to have worn a Scotland jersey. His record of 24 tries stood as a world record until 1987 when David Campese finally eclipsed it, and still stands as a Championship record.

Even if any Scot should ever beat Smith's total, no-one will come close to his strike rate of more than two in every three games (Tony Stanger, who also scored 24 tries for Scotland, took 52 Tests to do so). Even more importantly, given the importance of the Calcutta Cup, Smith scored nine tries in eight matches against the Auld Enemy.

'The Flying Scotsman' could play on the right or left wing and is remembered as part of the famous four-man Oxford University back division that formed the backbone of Scotland's 1925 Grand Slam-winning 'Immortals' side. He was arguably the most influential of the quartet, even more so than Phil MacPherson and certainly more so than Johnny Wallace or George Aitken. Indeed, in the first two matches of that season he scored a total of eight tries against France and Wales (including the last three against France and the first three against Wales), and while he barely touched the ball against England because he was so heavily marked, the space he created ensured Scotland went on to win the match.

The wing had already made everyone sit up and take notice when he first took up the sport at Oxford University, and by the time he walked off the Inverleith pitch after his debut for Scotland against Wales in 1924 no-one was under any illusions that he was a very special player indeed – he had scored a hat-trick as Scotland pulled away to 35–0 before taking their foot off the pedal in a match that finished 35–10.

Smith was the fastest of the Oxford University three-quarters; such was his pace that he was said to be a match for sprint contemporary Eric Liddell with the ball in hand. He was also a leader of men, and in 1933 he captained Scotland to a Triple Crown in Dublin, where they overcame ferocious Irish defence to win 8–6 as Harry Lind's late drop goal gave Scotland their first Triple Crown since 1925.

The one disappointment of Smith's career was the 1924 Lions tour to South Africa, where he injured himself and made just two appearances. Not that Smith ever let his infrequent disappointments get him down. A naturally exuberant character, there were endless stories of his carousing, the most famous concerning a post-match drinking binge which ended with him driving his car onto the pavement in Princes Street with His Majesty's Constabulary in hot pursuit.

Ian Smith's vital statistics
Caps: 33, (1924–33)
Position: Wing
Clubs: Oxford University, Edinburgh University, London Scottish

— SEVEN MINUTES OF WOE —

The quickest try conceded by Scotland came at Murrayfield, in the match against Italy in the 2007 Six Nations. It came when stand-off Phil Godman, making his first Championship start, received the ball from the breakdown after Scott Murray had fielded the Italian kick-off and tried to dink the ball over the head of the advancing openside Mauro Bergamasco. The Italian simply plucked the ball out of the air and rushed over for the opening try after just 18 seconds. If that was bad, though, scrum-half Chris Cuister then threw two passes that were intercepted and within seven minutes Scotland were 21–0 behind, eventually losing 37–17 to the Azzurri, for whom this was their first away win in the Six Nations.

Italy, of course, have become something of a bogey team for Scotland, who lost in Rome on Italy's Six Nations bow in 2000, when Scotland were the reigning Five Nations champions. They also beat Scotland in 2004 and 2007.

— HEINEKEN HEROES —

Seven Scots have played in Heineken Cup-winning sides. Craig Moir, Mattie Stewart, Budge Pountney and Donnie MacKinnon were in the starting XV when Northampton beat Munster by a single point at Twickenham in 2000, while Richard Metcalfe and Simon Holmes stayed on the bench.

Andy Nicol was the captain of a Bath side in which prop Dave Hilton was also present when the West Country side beat Brive in 1998, while Eric Peters stayed on the bench in that match.

Finally, in 2007, former Stirling County scrum-half Mark McMillan came off the bench when the Londoners beat old rivals Leicester in front of 85,000 fans at Twickenham. Former Boroughmuir and Leeds No.8 Stuart Reid came close to adding his name to the list when he captained Narbonne in the European Challenge Cup final in 2001 at Reading's Madjeski Stadium. However, his side were beaten 42–33 by Harlequins.

— WORLD CHAMPS? —

It wasn't just the 1967 Scotland football team which became proxy world champions by beating England under Wembley's Twin Towers; the Scotland rugby team did exactly the same against an unbeaten England rugby team, winning 8–5 at Wembley in May 1942.

— UMPIRE PUNISHES NOISY ENGLAND —

The scorer of the first try in international rugby was Angus Buchanan, who played for Edinburgh's Royal High School FP. During the first ever international in 1871, Scotland had pushed a scrum over the try-line and Buchanan had fallen on the ball.

The England players protested long and hard that the try wasn't good, but after he had heard the appeal the umpire let the try stand. In those days only goals, rather than tries, counted (scoring a try allowed a team to 'try' for a goal), but William Cross kicked a fine conversion for the only score of the match.

The umpire was the famous Loretto headmaster Dr Hely Hutchinson ('H.H.') Almond, who later wrote: "Let me make a confession: I do not know whether the decision which gave Scotland the try from which the winning goal was kicked was correct in fact. When an umpire is in doubt, I think he is justified in deciding against the side which makes the most noise. They are probably in the wrong."

— CROWD RECORD —

In 1973, when the Welsh were at the height of their powers and a young full back called Andy Irvine was setting Scottish pulses racing, the Five Nations match between the Scots and Welsh at Murrayfield set a northern hemisphere attendance record that still stands to this day. The estimated crowd for that day was 104,000, including 20,000 from Wales (a further 20,000 were locked out). The huge demand led to internationals at Murrayfield becoming all-ticket; before 1973 fans could pay on the door.

— KEN SAYS NO TO TOE —

Ken Scotland was the first regular Scotland place-kicker to favour the round-the-corner style rather than the toe punt favoured by specialists such as New Zealand's Don Clarke and South Africa's Bennie Osler. He was conspicuously successful during the 1959 tour to New Zealand.

— OLD RIVALS —

Edinburgh Academicals were the first club to be founded in Scotland in 1857. Their annual match against Merchiston Castle was first played in 1858 and is the oldest continuous fixture still in existence.

— MIX AND MATCH —

In the first ever mixed international, England-Wales beat Scotland-Ireland 21–16 in 1923 at Rugby School in a closed-doors match held to commemorate the centenary of William Webb-Ellis's decision to do a runner with the ball. Scottish international J.B. Bruce-Lockhart was a master at Rugby at the time and made most of the arrangements for the game to take place.

The Scots and Irish got their revenge six years later, though, when they beat the English and Welsh 20–13 at Twickenham in a match to commemorate the death of English administrator Sir George Rowland Hill. Further games saw Scotland-Ireland beat England-Wales 17–3 in the Red Cross game in 1939; England-Wales beat Scotland-Ireland 26–17 in 1959 in the Twickenham Rugby Jubilee; Scotland-Ireland beat England-Wales 21–20 in the 1972 SRU Centenary Match at Murrayfield, with the peerless Mike Gibson scoring a hat-trick of tries; in 1975 Ireland-Scotland beat England-Wales 17–10 during the IRFU's Centenary celebrations at Lansdowne Road in Dublin; finally, in 1980, Wales-England beat Scotland-Ireland 37–33 in Cardiff in the Welsh RU Centenary match.

— MISSED OPPORTUNITY —

Demonstrating an epic ability to launch toys from their pram, the SRU refused to invite the touring All Blacks to play at Murrayfield in 1925 because they were unwilling to allow the RFU alone to organise the tour.

Scotland would go on to win the Grand Slam that year with a team that included the famous Oxford University three-quarter line made up of right-wing Ian Smith, the New Zealand-raised 'Flying Scot' who scored four tries against both Wales and France, left-wing A.C. Wallace, who was later to skipper the Wallabies, and the two centres, captain G.P.S. MacPherson and G.G. Aitken, the Rhodes Scholar who had already captained New Zealand.

That was a Scotland team which may well have beaten All Blacks skipper Cliff Porter's 'Invincibles' – instead, they went home unbeaten while Scottish rugby fans missed out on the chance to see the peerless Maori full back George Nepia play.

— WORLD-CLASS DUO —

Andy Nicol and Gavin Hastings were the only Scots to play for the Rest of the World against the All Blacks in the NZRFU's centenary matches in 1992.

— SPORTING ALL-ROUNDER —

Scotland's answer to C.B. Fry, England's dashing footballer, cricketer, rugby player and world long jump record holder of the late 1800s and early 1900s, was a young man of the Edwardian era called K.G. MacLeod, an unstoppable runner and a sublime kicker of the ball who scored a breathtaking try against the 1906 Springboks.

A sporting prodigy, he was only 17 and still at Fettes College when he was picked to play against New Zealander Dave Gallacher's 1905 'Originals'. That was the first of the centre's nine caps, all of them won before he graduated from Cambridge University. Sadly for the game in general and for Scottish rugby in particular, MacLeod finally gave in to his father – who begged him to give up the game which had seriously injured his two older brothers – and hung up his boots before his 21st birthday, long before he had matured as a player.

A glimpse of what might have been came in his sporting career once he had retired from rugby: he had already been Scottish long jump champion, but he went on to captain Lancashire at cricket, play football for Manchester City and, in middle-age, win the Amateur Golf Championship of Natal.

Not that MacLeod was the only genuine talent to be immune to the call of Murrayfield. Despite captaining Scotland and being feted after scoring the deciding try in Scotland's famous 1923 win over Wales in Cardiff, A.L. Gracie quickly fell out of love with the game. Selected for the national trial in 1924/25 and then for the Five Nations game against France, he simply informed the selectors that he was no longer interested.

— TALENTED DOC —

Dr Kevin O'Flanagan, Arsenal's leading goalscorer in 1946, played football for Ireland against Scotland in Belfast in the first weekend in February, and rugby for Ireland against Scotland at Lansdowne Road the following week.

— LORDING IT —

Only one serving nobleman has played for Scotland, but he did so with distinction. Lord John M. Bannerman retired at the tender age of 27, but he did so after winning 38 consecutive caps, a record that was unsurpassed until overtaken by Hawick's Hugh McLeod in 1962.

— TV FIRST —

Wilson Shaw: Scotland rugby's first TV star

The first televised Scotland international was the 1938 Calcutta Cup at Twickenham, although the only people who could get reception lived within 20 miles of London. Scotland won 21–16 to win the Triple Crown despite being totally overwhelmed in the forwards, a win largely ascribed to the genius of Glasgow High School FP fly-half Wilson Shaw.

— MOVING THE GOALPOSTS —

There was once a joint Gala-Melrose club, until one day the Gala men turned up to discover that the goalposts had been moved to Melrose.

— THE FOOT-RUSH —

For a long time, the glory of Scottish forward play was the foot-rush, the controlled dribble, either from a wheeled scrum or from broken play, to the roar of "feet, Scotland, feet". Changes in the laws of the game, in the composition of the ball itself and in fashion have long made the foot-rush obsolete, although it was practised by Scottish packs as late as the 1950s, and schoolboys in that decade still spent many hours learning the art of dribbling.

— DRUNK IN CHARGE OF A MAIL CART —

After the 1873 match in Glasgow (a boring no-score draw) one of the English forwards got so drunk that he stole a mail cart and drove around the city.

— TWO SKIPPERS —

In 1937, Edinburgh Wanderers supplied both captains in a Scotland versus Wales match, the Scottish one, Ross Logan, being a Merchistonian, the Welsh one, V.I. Rees, being a centre. Scotland won 13–6 in Swansea.

— LINGUISTIC CONFUSION —

In 1938, when Wales travelled north to Murrayfield, they brought 10,000 supporters with them. So many were from West Wales and could not speak English that the London Midland and Scottish train company employed only Welsh-speaking guards.

— ENGLAND DOUBLE —

1971 was a year of unbounded joy for Scotland in their relations with the Auld Enemy. Not only did they win 16–15 at Twickenham, their first win at the Cabbage Patch for 33 years, but the following Saturday they also beat the red rose mob 16–6 at Murrayfield in a match to commemorate the exact centenary of the first Raeburn Place match, thereby beating England twice in a fortnight.

Even better, England's heavy 23–9 Five Nations defeat the following year at Murrayfield gave them their first Wooden Spoon. Just to rub salt into the wounds, Scotland-Ireland also beat England-Wales 20–21 at Murrayfield in the 1972 SRU Centenary Match.

— SCOTLAND LEGENDS XV: G.P.S. MACPHERSON —

G.P.S. MacPherson: Scotland's greatest ever player?

Norman Mair, player-coach-journalist and all-round venerable sage of Scottish rugby, reckons that MacPherson was the best player to ever play for Scotland. Whether or not that is true will always be open to debate, but there is plenty of evidence to suggest that he was a player of rare quality.

The Grand Slam-winning captain with the 1925 'Immortals', who completed their clean sweep with a nailbitingly close 14–11 win over the Auld Emeny at the newly-opened Murrayfield, MacPherson was the most outrageously talented attacking centre of his generation, and probably any other. A player who could jink his way through heavy traffic, selling dummies as he went, he was never a particularly strong tackler but few got past him either.

After making his debut against France in 1922 he was already a legend in the making when he teamed up with Oxford University team-mates Aitken, Wallace and Smith for Scotland in 1924, but it was his partnership with Ian Smith that was to transform him from rugby demi-god to fully-fledged deity. In 17 matches together over eight seasons, the pair scored 29 of Scotland's 49 tries, their most prolific phase coming when Smith switched to the left wing for the 1925 Grand Slam season, a year when they scored eight of Scotland's 15 tries.

An urbane, modest and intelligent man, MacPherson went on to become vice-president of the investment bank Kleinwort Benson from 1961–69.

G.P.S. MacPherson vital statistics
Caps: 26 (1922–32)
Position: Centre
Clubs: Oxford University, Edinburgh Academicals

— BIG WIN, HEAVY DEFEAT —

One of Scotland's best ever results and arguably their worst ever defeat came in the same year, 1951, in the middle of a dire run for the Scotland team. In February, in front of an 80,000 crowd swollen by the arrival of 25,000 Welshmen, a little-fancied Scotland upset a legendary Welsh side chasing their second Triple Crown in succession, winning 19–0 with Doug Elliot and Peter Kininmonth particularly outstanding.

In November of that same year, Scotland sustained a savage defeat against a Springboks side which had been beaten by London a fortnight earlier, shipping nine tries as South Africa won an embarrassingly one-sided match by 44–0. The defeat is believed to be the origin of the phrase "and they were lucky to get nought" and was the start of a 17-match losing streak that saw Scotland go for an incredible four years without a win. During that dismal run Scotland scored just 54 points: 11 tries, six conversions, and four penalties.

The largest points margin by which Scotland have lost a game at Murrayfield is also against South Africa – a 68–10 beating in 1998. However, tries were worth five points by then, while the 44–0 loss in 1951 would become 62–0 under the 1998 scoring system.

— SCOTLAND LEGENDS XV: FINLAY CALDER —

Grand Slam hero Finlay Calder

Tough, uncompromising and fiercely competitive, Finlay Calder followed his twin brother Jim into the history books by becoming a Grand Slam-winning international when Scotland famously beat England in 1990. Not only that, but he led the Lions to Australia in 1989 and returned victorious, and played in the first two World Cups, being one of the prime movers as Scotland achieved the fourth-place finish in 1991 that remains their best result at the game's showpiece tournament.

But it could all have been so different. Even more so than Ian McLauchlan, Finlay Calder came late to international rugby, making his debut in 1986 at the age of 28. Only the year before he had been on the brink of retiring and abandoning his dream of following brother Jim into the Scotland team when Jim Telfer suggested he move to openside. Despite lacking the pace of an out-and-out openside, Calder took his advice and the rest is history.

And what a history. In those five short years at the top, Calder managed to pack in more incident than many players who had spent twice as long playing for their country. In his first year with Scotland he was part of a team that shared the Championship, but at the 1987 World Cup defeat by France meant running into an All Blacks side on top form. According to coach Brian Lochore, beating a side as good as Scotland 30–3 was the moment at which they thought they could go all the way. Lochore singled Calder out for special mention.

The highest point of Calder's career was becoming the first Scot to captain the British Lions since Mike Campbell-Lamerton in 1966 and the first captain of a winning Lions side since Willie John McBride in 1974. An intense man whose seven caps as captain of Scotland had laid bare his desperate drive to win on the park and his winning bonhomie off it, Calder was the perfect man for the job of leading a disparate group of players into Australia. Despite losing the First Test, he simply drafted in a raft of English forwards and did what was necessary to win the Second and Third Tests, even if their occasionally brutal play didn't win many friends Down Under.

Not that Calder was worried about making friends once he crossed the whitewash, as he showed in 1990 and 1991. It was all about doing whatever he needed to win. In 1990, he was in the thick of the battle against England and put in a rampaging never-say-die performance that knocked the visitors out of their stride and helped secure the Grand Slam. In 1991, after being coaxed out of retirement by Jim Telfer, his World Cup will be remembered for his history-altering stiff-arm on Ireland's Jim Staples and allegations of a headbutt on All Black hooker Sean Fitzpatrick.

None of that will bother Calder, who will probably regard those instances as mere collateral damage and say that if he has one overriding regret about his career, it is that he never got to play alongside his brother Jim for Scotland. Jim won all of his 27 caps between 1981–85, including scoring the Grand Slam-securing try in 1984 and touring with the Lions in 1983. Finlay did, however, get to appear alongside Jim in a Scotland shirt when the twins and older brother John all toured Australia with Scotland in 1982 (a fourth brother was also a quality player, with Gavin, John, Jim and Finlay all representing Scottish Schools).

Finlay Calder vital statistics
Caps: 34 (1986–91)
Position: Flanker
Club: Stewart's-Melville FP

— SCOTLAND AT THE WORLD CUP:
1991, FIVE NATIONS —

After coming to within a whisker of beating New Zealand the previous summer, Scotland had stuttered in the Five Nations. Then a Scotland XV was beaten on the road by Canada and Romania in two of their warm-up games, drawing the other with a handy Barbarians side. Once the tournament started, however, Scotland crushed a spirited Japanese 47–9, overran Zimbabwe 51–12 and then overcame Ireland 24–15 at Murrayfield in a match that was nail-bitingly close until Finlay Calder controversially took out Irish full back Jim Staples while he was fielding a Gary Armstrong garryowen. The groggy Staples – Ireland said Calder had forearm smashed him, which the Scot denied – spilled the ball and young replacement fly-half Graham Shiel went over for a try on his debut.

In the quarter-final, Scotland faced the Western Samoa side which had beaten hosts Wales, crushed Argentina and come within a score of beating Australia, but with Gavin Hastings acting as a battering ram close to the pack, Scotland were unstoppable and two John Jeffrey tries saw them win 28–6.

The semi-final against England at Murrayfield – the first meeting between the two in Edinburgh since the 1990 Grand Slam decider – was incredibly fraught, with Scotland hanging on despite the dominance of England's pack. The crucial moment came late in the game, with the scores tied at 6–6, when Gavin Hastings got a penalty in front of the posts but inexplicably pulled it wide from almost point blank range.

Rob Andrew's late drop goal settled the affair, and Scotland finished the tournament losing the 3rd/4th-place play-off against the All Blacks in Cardiff, going down 13–6 with centre Walter Little scoring the only try of the game.

Pool matches:
Scotland 47 Japan 9
Scotland 51 Zimbabwe 12
Scotland 24 Ireland 15

Quarter-final:
Scotland 28 Western Samoa 6

Semi-final
Scotland 6 England 9

3rd/4th Play-off
Scotland 6 New Zealand 13.

— GRANNYGATE —

In 2000, just six days before Scotland were due to play Wales in Cardiff in the Six Nations, Glasgow's *Sunday Herald* newspaper revealed that two of Wales's New Zealand-born players had no qualifications to play for their adopted country. Both had said they had Welsh grandmothers and both had been taken on trust. 'Grannygate' had arrived.

Full back Shane Howarth and open-side flanker Brett Sinkinson were eventually disqualified from playing for Wales, but the identification of an obvious loophole in the regulations – basically that the authorities took it on trust that if a player said he was qualified to play for a country, then it must be true – prompted a witchhunt to see if any other players in other countries had been breaking the rules.

The only two other capped players who were also found to have broken the rules were two Englishmen who had both been representing Scotland. One was Alnwick farmer Peter Walton, who had been at boarding school north of the border, had represented Scottish Schools and who genuinely thought he qualified to play for his adopted country. He had won 23 caps, but had retired the previous year after the 1999 World Cup.

It was a different matter with Bath prop Dave Hilton, who had won 41 caps on the loosehead for Scotland. For a start, the Bristolian butcher's son was still playing, basing his eligibility on having a maternal grandfather born in Edinburgh. Embarrassingly, when checked it turned out that his grandfather Walter was born in, er, Bristol.

"Both myself and my father had always believed that my grandfather Walter was born in Edinburgh," Hilton said at the time. "I was absolutely devastated when my family completed their research to discover that was, in fact, not the case. He was actually born in Bristol and it was the first that any of us in the family knew of this. I regard myself as Scottish and I am immensely proud to have won 41 caps for Scotland."

It was a story with a happy ending, however. In 2002, and by now a Glasgow player qualified for his adopted country by dint of living and playing north of the border for the requisite three years, the 32-year-old made his comeback as a replacement in the 21–6 win over the Springboks at Murrayfield. It was, however, to be his 42nd and final cap. At least his son won't have the same problem: born in Glasgow, he was christened "Scott".

— SCOTLAND'S GREATEST GAMES 3 —

Scotland 21 France 12
Murrayfield
17th March 1984

Unbeaten Scotland had been exceptional on the way to their showdown with France at Murrayfield, and although the French had drawn in Dublin, they were still determined to claim the Championship by winning at Murrayfield. For much of the first half, it looked as if that was exactly what would happen. Despite conceding nine penalties in a row at one stage, the French dominated and it was no surprise when playmaker and scrum-half Jerome Gallion burrowed his way over for a deserved try.

Although Peter Dods kicked a penalty to make it 6–3 at half-time, Jean-Patrick Lescaboura extended France's lead straight after the interval as the visitors looked good value for their lead. But when David Leslie and Gallion had a clash of heads chasing a loose ball, the tide began to turn. With their leader Gallion stretchered off, the French began to fray around the edges, and nowhere was that more obvious than when they argued so vociferously with the referee over one penalty that he moved it from an unkickable 50 metres to an entirely kickable 40 metres, and Dods moved Scotland to within three points of the visitors.

When Dods kicked Scotland level, France looked visibly shaken. Although Lescaboura dropped an enormous goal, Dods responded at once (despite having one eye so swollen it was almost shut, he would score 17 points to equal Andy Irvine's Five Nations record) and for the first time the match looked to be in the balance.

Serge Blanco was infected by the French jitters and when he made a mess of fielding a high ball, he was swept 25 yards upfield before being bundled into touch just short of the French line. Colin Deans threw long to Iain Paxton, but Jean-Luc Joinel got his hand to the ball, palming it back only to then see that Jim Calder had anticipated where the ball would land and Fin Calder's twin brother dropped over for the try that broke the French resistance. A conversion and late penalty from Dods meant that Scotland had scored 18 points in the final 14 minutes for a famous Grand Slam-winning victory.

— REPELLING THE FRENCH INVADERS —

Scotland's first Murrayfield defeat to France didn't come until 1952, a quarter of a century after the two nations first met at the new stadium in 1927.

— FIRST TOUR —

Scotland were the first major nation ever to undertake an overseas tour, travelling to South Africa in 1960, where they lost to an experimental Springboks side 18–10 in Port Elizabeth. They did, however, beat Griqualand West 21–11 and East Transvaal 30–16.

— PAYING RESPECT —

When Scotland played France at Murrayfield in 1968, all the players wore black armbands to mark the deaths in two separate car crashes of centre Guy Boniface and wing Michel Capendeguy.

— MURRAYFIELD SEVENS —

The first international sevens tournament was held at Murrayfield in 1973, with England's Keith Fielding, a future star of the television programme *Superstars*, stealing the show shortly before heading off to Rugby League. The next time what was effectively a Sevens World Cup was staged at Murrayfield was in 1993, with an England team led by Andrew Harriman again taking the honours.

— FIRST TITLE FOR HAWICK —

In 1974, Hawick won the first club championship in Britain and Ireland. Despite losing 13–9 at Mansfield Park to a West of Scotland side containing legends like McHarg and Brown, Hawick beat West to the first title on points difference.

— POWERFUL CONNECTIONS —

Scotland wing Bill Gammell was a uniquely influential man at the start of the new millennium. Not only did he go to school with his close friend Tony Blair, but thanks to his father's role as a prominent oilman, he spent his summers holidaying with two future US presidents, George Bush Snr and Jnr. Gammell, whose oil company Cairn Energy is one of Scotland's most successful businesses, became Sir Bill in Blair's final honours list.

— IRVINE'S RECORD —

In 1981 Andy Irvine was the first Scottish player ever to hold the world record for points scored. His four penalties in Scotland's 12–6 win over Romania at Murrayfield took him to 209 points, overtaking the legendary All Black Don Clarke's tally of 207.

— GUEST SUCCESS —

The only two post-war guest sides to win the Middlesex Sevens were both from Scotland: Stewart's-Melville FP and Andy Irvine's Heriot's FP.

— CLOSE . . . BUT NO CIGAR —

Scotland player and coach Jim Telfer had huge admiration for the All Blacks and it was his dearest wish to see his country beat the Kiwis. Although that never happened under his watch, he played in the 0–0 1964 draw at Murrayfield, and then had to watch in 1983 as Peter Dods missed a last-minute touchline conversion with the scores tied at 25–25. He later said that the Test defeat in 1990, when Scotland were clearly the better side at Eden Park but lost 21–18 despite outscoring the Kiwis by two tries to one, was the saddest day of his coaching career.

— HUMILIATED BY THE MINNOWS —

Scotland's worst results against so-called minnows:

- Scotland have twice lost to Romania in Bucharest: 28–22 in 1984 after leading 19–12 with 15 minutes remaining, and 18–12 in 1991.
- Japan beat Scotland 28–24 in Tokyo 1989.
- In 1993 Scotland lost 21–10 to Western Samoa in Apia.
- The following year they lost 18–16 to Canada and 16–15 to Argentina in successive matches.
- In 1997 Scotland were hammered 51–16 by Fiji in Suva.

— FIRST FOR IRVINE —

The first man ever to be awarded a penalty try was Scotland's Andy Irvine, against Wales in 1981.

— NO.8 SURPLUS —

Scotland are the only side ever to have started a Test match with four No.8s. Derek White played in the second row, Finlay Calder at open-side flanker, John Jeffrey at blind-side and Iain Paxton at No.8 when Scotland played Romania and France in the pool matches in the opening World Cup in 1987. Hawick No.8 Derek Turnbull replaced Jeffrey in the 30–3 quarter-final loss to eventual winners New Zealand. Scotland thus played five first-choice club No.8s in the 1987 World Cup.

— CHAMPION PROS —

The SRU may have been caught unawares and unprepared by the onset of professionalism immediately after the 1995 World Cup, but Scottish players were at the vanguard of professional rugby. Doddie Weir, George Graham, Alan Tait and Gary Armstrong all joined Scotland flanker Peter Walton at Rob Andrew's Newcastle Falcons when the north-east club became the first champions of the 'open' era in 1995.

— ANYONE BUT ENGLAND —

After the Lions tour of 1989, the Grand Slam decider of 1990 and the World Cup semi-final of 1991 left a mutual antipathy between several senior Scottish and English players. David Sole, John Jeffrey and Gavin Hastings turned up for the 1991 World Cup final at Twickenham between England and Australia wearing kilts . . . and Wallaby shirts.

— WAINRIGHT IN A DAZE —

The aftermath of the 1996 Calcutta Cup, won by England at Murrayfield, was dominated by allegations that Scotland's key player, skipper Rob Wainwright, was punched in an early maul by visiting prop Jason Leonard and spent the rest of the game in a daze. Wainwright didn't see who hit him but flanker Ian Smith confirmed later that Wainwright had received a blow to the head.

"I asked Rob if he was okay," said Smith. "He looked at me and asked me who I was and what time it was. I took it from that that he wasn't."

— TEAPOT'S TAP DANCE —

Scotland tighthead prop Peter Wright had a mixed Calcutta Cup in 1996. Nicknamed 'Teapot' by amused Kiwi fans during the Lions tour of New Zealand in 1993 due to his habit of walking everywhere with his hands on his hips, Wright was fined £2,000 by the SRU for breaches of contract – £1,000 for failing to meet fitness standards set by the coach and £1,000 for tap dancing on Dean Richards' head in the Calcutta Cup.

— THREE BROTHERS —

The three Milne brothers, Iain, Kenny and David, all represented Scotland between 1979 and 1991 but the trio never played together. Indeed, David won his only cap as a replacement prop playing alongside hooker Kenny against Japan in the 1991 World Cup at Murrayfield a year after injury had forced his brother Iain 'The Bear' Milne to hang up his boots. Kenny and Iain won 44 and 40 caps respectively, but only played together twice, against Wales in 1989 and in the Second Test in New Zealand in 1990.

There have only been two cases where three brothers have played on the same international team, one where three Scots played together and one where Scotland were the opponents.

In 1875, when Scotland fought out an entertaining 0–0 draw with England at Raeburn Place, the three Finlay brothers, James, Arthur and Ninian, were key components of the Scotland side. James was winning the last of his four caps, while Arthur and Ninian were winning their first caps – Ninian was still a schoolboy, but was such an incredibly powerful runner and sublime drop-kicker that he soon became the first real superstar of Scottish rugby and went on to win nine caps, playing until 1881.

In November 1912 the Springboks fielded Freddie, Dick and John Luyt in the side that beat Scotland 16–0.

— VETERAN INTERNATIONAL —

Mac Henderson, capped three times in 1933, became Scotland's oldest living international and the first to become a centenarian when he celebrated his 100th birthday on 1st May 2007.

— SCOTLAND'S GREATEST GAMES 4 —

New Zealand 21 Scotland 18
Eden Park, Auckland
23rd June 1990

In 24 attempts up to the 2007 World Cup, Scotland have never beaten New Zealand. They might have done had they been willing to play the 1925 'Invincibles' when at their peak, but the SRU in its wisdom refused to host the incoming tour. There have been two draws between the sides – the 0–0 draw at Murrayfield in 1964 when Jim Telfer's men not only prevented the All Blacks completing a Grand Slam tour but constantly threatened to cross the star-studded visitors' line; and the 25–25 draw in 1983 when Jim Pollock's try gave Peter Dods a chance to kick a last-second conversion which would have won the game.

Yet however thrilling those two games undoubtedly were, the Second Test in 1990 was an even better game. Not only did Scotland outscore the All Blacks by two tries to one (as opposed to being outscored 3–1 in 1983), but they also did so in the world champions' back yard in compelling fashion at a time when New Zealand were considered virtually unbeatable.

Indeed, had it not been for a combination of All Black fly-half Grant Fox kicking six penalties from six attempts and some highly dubious refereeing from Southern Hemisphere-loving Welshman Derek Bevan (yes, he of gold watch fame), Scotland would undoubtedly have secured the most famous win in their history.

After having been soundly beaten in the First Test in Dunedin, the visitors deservedly pulled away through two penalties from Gavin Hastings and a converted try from Tony Stanger to just one penalty to give them an early 12–3 lead. With half-time in sight, a fine try from Alex Moore put the Scots 18–9 ahead.

Yet Scotland had almost gone ahead too early, and the All Blacks began to peg them back. A Fox penalty before half-time made it 18–12, but the pivotal moment of the game came in the second half at 18–15 when Kieron Crowley punted long to Gavin Hastings, who slipped and was pounced upon by flanker Mike Brewer who had been lurking in an offside position. Bevan ignored that though, instead penalising the full back for failing to release. Fox kicked the three points before applying the *coup de grâce* with just minutes remaining.

— SCOTLAND LEGENDS XV: GORDON BROWN —

Broon frae Troon!

Where to start with the 'Broon frae Troon'? A larger-then-life bear of a man who remained a major rugby figure well beyond his playing days largely by dint of an infectious love of life that found an outlet on the after-dinner speaking circuit and latterly in the television commentary booth, Brown was something of a national institution when he succumbed to cancer at the tragically early age of 53.

Yet he wasn't loved by those who had to face him on a rugby field in his prime. Almost certainly Scotland's greatest tight forward of all time, Brown was as uncompromising on the pitch as he was gentle and friendly off it. He wasn't just a hardman though: the younger brother of fellow international Peter and the son of international football goalkeeper Jock, Gordon was an athletic big man who was surprisingly mobile, a superb scrummager and a top lineout forward.

After making his debut in the 6–3 win over South Africa in 1969, the 6ft 5in 17 stone colossus quickly established himself alongside a group of uncompromising Scottish forwards such as Alistair McHarg, Sandy

Carmichael, P.C. Brown, Rodger Arneil and Ian McLauchlan, who were collectively known as the Mean Machine. However, Brown wasn't an assiduous trainer and his sporadic appearances at training meant that he reserved his best displays for the long Lions tours where fitness training was incremental and unavoidable. Brown's outgoing nature was also perfect for a tour like the Lions, where there is a need for former opponents to mesh quickly, and he was recognised as a tourist par excellence.

It is for his displays with the Lions, particularly the 1974 team, that Brown will always be remembered. He squeaked into the squad for the 1971 Lions tour to New Zealand and performed so well that he forced his way into the second row alongside Willie John McBride for the final two Tests.

The tour party that arrived in New Zealand in 1971 was arguably the best that ever left these shores, so to get into the Test team was no mean feat. But it was three years later in South Africa in 1974, where he scored eight tries in 12 matches, including two in the Tests (he never scored a try for Scotland) that he indelibly seared himself into the national consciousness. Perhaps it was because the tour was televised, or perhaps because it was punctuated by telegenic bouts of on-field fisticuffs that were to go down in the annals of history, but either way the public at home saw what an effective operator Brown was at the very highest level, and what a devastating brawler he could be when push came to shove come the '99' call.

Brown is one of the elite band of players to be picked for a third Lions tour when he travelled with the 1977 squad to New Zealand, but by then he was 30 years old and had won his 30th and final cap for Scotland the year before, and he never got near the Test team.

Gordon Brown vital statistics
Caps: 30 (1969–76)
Position: Second row
Club: West of Scotland

— SPORTING FAMILY —

Apart from being a father-son combination who played for Scotland (see *Like Father, Like Son*, page 141), Max and Brian Simmers' family has a couple of other sporting connections. Max's mother-in-law and Brian's grandmother was Charlotte Cooper, five-times Wimbledon singles champion in 1895, 1896, 1898, 1901 and 1908. Meanwhile, Charlotte's daughter (and Max's wife) Gwen was also a very good tennis player, appearing in the Wightman Cup.

— SCOTTISH POWER —

The clubs who have provided the greatest number of Scottish internationals:

> London Scottish: 135
> Edinburgh Accies: 76
> Hawick: 58

— ONE CAP WONDERS —

Two hundred players have won single caps for Scotland in 558 full cap internationals played over 136 years. The first international was played on 27th March 1871 and eight players from the victorious 20 did not play again for Scotland. Indeed, a total of 32 players won single caps in the 11 internationals played during the 1870s. And half of all single cappers played during the 43-year period prior to the First World War.

With the introduction of replacements and the professional era the number of players winning single caps has reduced significantly and since the turn of this century only Andrew Dall (2003), Scott Gray (2004), Andrew Hall (2002) and Andrew Wilson (2005) have won single caps.

— THRASHED! —

The biggest beating in Scottish pro-team rugby was Cardiff's 80–16 demolition of Edinburgh Reivers on 2nd September 2000 in Cardiff, Frank Hadden's first league match in charge of the Scottish club. Cardiff's coach that day was Lynn Howells who later succeeded Hadden as Edinburgh coach.

— OFF, OFF, OFF! —

Scotland players to be sent off:

- Nathan Hines v USA in the 65–23 victory in San Francisco on 22nd June 2002
- Scott Murray v Wales at the Millennium Stadium in the 28–18 defeat on 12th February 2006

Players sent off against Scotland:
Colin Meads (New Zealand), Murrayfield 1967
Alain Carmanati (France), Murrayfield, 1990
Massimo Giovanelli (Italy), Murrayfield, 1999

SCOTLAND
SHIRTS
1871–2009

1871   1900   Traditional

Traditional   1995 World Cup   1996-98

1996-98   1998-2000   1998-2000

1999 World Cup

1999 World Cup

2000-03

2000-03

2003-05

2003-05

2003 World cup

2005-07

2005-07

2007

2007-09

2007-09

2007 World Cup

2007 World Cup

— SCOTLAND'S GREATEST GAMES 5 —

England 3 Scotland 9
Richmond
7th March 1891

This match had shades of 1990 about it – unbeaten visitors playing unbeaten but less impressive hosts in a winner-takes-all Calcutta Cup showdown for the highest honour then available in the game. In this case, however, the match was being played for the Triple Crown, was being held in England and the Scots were the form team.

Scotland had already thrashed Wales and Ireland by 15–0 and 14–0 respectively (a healthy win in the days when a try was worth two points) while England had not been quite as impressive in registering their two wins, but despite that 20,000 spectators turned up at Richmond in the hope of seeing England take the Triple Crown.

They were to be sorely disappointed as Scotland went on to win their first Triple Crown in the rain with an utterly dominant display from their forwards and halfbacks that prevented their hosts unleashing their highly dangerous back division.

The Scots were quick off the mark with stand-off Charles Orr, part of a large West of Scotland contingent, combining with Gregor MacGregor to give wing Peter Clauss enough space to drop a goal within five minutes of the start.

There was no more scoring in that half but the second period started in similar style, with MacGregor working prop John Orr (one of two sets of brothers, the others being George and Willie Neilson) over for a try. MacGregor made the third score too, his floated pass putting Willie Neilson in for the try that settled the matter despite Richard Lockwood's late score.

Scotland had travelled south and destroyed the English, wresting the Triple Crown from their grasp and leaving the huge crowd to depart in sullen silence. Rugby anoraks should note that this was also the last match played before the introduction of the penalty (until that stage, infringements had been punished with a scrum restart).

— BENCH RECORD —

The player who spent the most time on the bench without being capped is Rob Cunningham. Incredibly, he was an unused sub for every match bar one of Colin Deans' 52 caps – that's 51 times collecting splinters without ever getting a single cap.

— SEQUENCES —

- During a 27-year period between 1923 and 1950 France lost all seven matches played in Scotland: two at Inverleith and five at Murrayfield. They finally recorded their second ever win in Scotland on 14th January 1950, winning 8–5 at Murrayfield.
- Scotland were unbeaten by Ireland from 1989–1999, winning 11 and drawing one of the 12 matches, including a Rugby World Cup pool match in 1991. The remarkable run finally came to an end when Ireland won 44–22 at Lansdowne Road on 19th February 2000.

— BETE NOIRES —

The players to have scored the most points in a single match against Scotland:

Diego Dominguez (Italy): 29 points (6 penalties, 3 drop goals) in the 34–20 win at Stadio Flaminio on 5th February 2000

Jonny Wilkinson (England): 27 points (1 try, 2 conversions, 5 penalties, 1 drop goal) in the 42–20 win at Twickenham in 2007

Rob Andrew (England): 24 points (7 penalties, 1 drop goal) in the 24–12 win at Twickenham on 18th March 1995

Jason Leonard (England) has been on the longest winning sequence against Scotland appearing in the England side which won ten consecutive matches between 1991 and 1999.

— MOST TRIES AGAINST SCOTLAND —

Jonah Lomu (New Zealand): 7 tries in six Tests (1995–2001)
Tana Umaga (New Zealand): 7 tries in five Tests (1999–2005)
Christian Cullen (New Zealand): 6 tries in five Tests, including four in his first Test against Scotland (1996–2000)
Gareth Edwards (Wales): 6 tries in 11 Tests (1967–1978)
Ken Jones (Wales): 6 tries in ten Tests (1947–1957)
Cyril Lowe (England): 6 tries in six Tests (1913–1925)

— THE BORDERS LEAGUE —

The Borders league came about in 1901/02 and remains the oldest league in rugby.

The working-class clubs in the Borders resented the control of the FP (former pupils) clubs in Edinburgh and Glasgow – no player from a Borders club had been capped until Gala's Adam Dalgleish was selected to play Wales in 1890 – and several times almost followed the lead of the clubs in the north of England by breaking away from the Scottish Rugby Union. However, they stayed in the fold and to satisfy their desire for meaningful competitive rugby, they were allowed to start a league by an SRU which viewed such a concept with disdain.

The original members of the Borders League were Gala, Hawick, Langholm, Melrose and JedForest. In 1912, Kelso and Selkirk brought the number up to seven, and in 1996, after decades of lobbying, Peebles were also allowed entry. Berwick and Duns followed later, although the latter's prolonged involvement is threatened by a lack of playing numbers.

Hawick remain the team with the greatest number of Border League titles, having won 49 by the end of the 2007 season, which they ended by defeating Selkirk. The other winners are Melrose (17 titles), JedForest (10), Gala (8), Kelso (5), Selkirk (3) and Langholm (1).

— TRAGEDY ON TOUR —

Scotland refused to allow its players to take part in the first British Isles touring side in 1888, believing the side to be tainted by professionalism. That team toured New Zealand and Australia, where its original captain R.L. Seddon drowned in the Hunter River and was replaced by England cricket cap A.E. Stoddart.

When it came to the second such tour, the SRU wholeheartedly embraced the concept, and when in 1891 a British team left for South Africa, it was captained by a Scot, Bill Maclagan. The side won all 19 matches, including three against the Springboks and ended up with an impressive points aggregate of 224 points for and one against.

— PAYING YOUR OWN WAY —

In the early internationals, all players had to pay for their own travel and accommodation. Third-class travel was the norm, as was providing your own socks and shorts. Players representing Scotland were given one jersey which had to last them for their whole playing career.

— THE FIRST FULL BACK —

The first man to play as a single full back was a Scot, H.H. Johnston, who pioneered the position in 1877 against Ireland.

— MR CONSISTENCY —

The Scots who have played most consecutive Test matches:

Sandy Carmichael: 49 consecutive tests 1967–1978
Carmichael was first capped against Ireland on 25th February 1967.

Hugh McLeod: Won a total of 40 caps 1954–62 and did not miss a match during this period.

John Bannerman: Won all of his 37 caps consecutively between 1921–29, which included a Grand Slam and Triple Crown in 1925.

Tony Stanger: Won his first 35 caps consecutively between 1989–1994, scoring 15 of his 24 Test tries during this period, and most famously Scotland's only try in the 1990 Grand Slam decider at Murrayfield.

— NOT BOTHERING THE SCORERS —

Scotland have scored zero in 55 matches against the following countries:

Wales: 16 times
England: 14 times
Ireland: 14 times
France: six times
New Zealand: three times

Included in these figures are ten matches which were 0–0 draws (five v England, three v Ireland, one each v Wales and New Zealand).

Scotland once drew consecutive matches 0–0. This was in 1900 against Ireland at Lansdowne Road and two weeks later against England at Inverleith. The most recent 0–0 was against New Zealand in 1964.

— THE FIRST CALCUTTA CUP —

The first match for the Calcutta Cup took place in 1879 and resulted in a draw. Scotland scored one dropped goal and England scored one goal as the two sides did battle at Raeburn Place on 10th March.

England had to wait until 1883, some 12 years after the first match between the two nations, to register their first win on Scottish soil. This was finally achieved during what is generally accepted as the first year of the International Championship, which became the Five Nations Championship when France joined it in 1910. In front of 10,000 spectators, the far heavier England side triumphed by two tries to one, with the legendary Alan Rotherham dominating, and went on to win their first Triple Crown.

— 100 PLUS —

Players who have scored 100 points or more for Scotland:

Player	Points
Gavin Hastings	667
Chris Paterson	559
Andy Irvine	273
Kenny Logan	220
Peter Dods	210
Craig Chalmers	166
Gregor Townsend	164
Brendan Laney	141
Duncan Hodge	123
Tony Stanger	106

— BUSY DAY —

England forward John Henry Clayton prepared for the first ever international in 1871 by running four miles every morning before breakfast while his Newfoundland dog (like a St Bernard, only bigger!) made the pace. The 17-stone forward would then saddle up his horse and ride four miles to his office in Liverpool where he would do a 12-hour day before riding home to a dinner of rare beef and beer. Even so, accounts of the Raeburn Park match talk of Scotland's superior fitness.

— SCOTLAND AT THE WORLD CUP: 1995, SOUTH AFRICA —

Scotland cruised through the opening games, beating tournament whipping boys Ivory Coast 89–0, with Gavin Hastings scoring 44 points, and then dispatching Tonga 41–5, with Hastings scoring 31 of the points this time. As in 1987, their clash with France, this time their final pool match, once again turned out to be the vital fixture.

The match was nip and tuck from beginning to end, but just as Scotland looked as if they would win and avoid a quarter-final meeting with the All Blacks, Toulouse wing Emile Ntamack popped up to score one of the best tries of all time: with the ball passing through six pairs of hands and the French knowing that if it went dead they would lose, he rode two tackles and went over in the corner for a heartbreaking try that made the score 22–19.

That defeat meant that Scotland faced New Zealand in the first knock-out round in Loftus Versfeld, Pretoria, and once again they were to exit the competition at the hands of the All Blacks. Jonah Lomu had run every other team ragged, and had beaten England virtually single-handedly, but it was the All Blacks' all-round excellence which did for a plucky Scotland side, with Lomu being joined on the scoresheet by Sean Fitzpatrick, Andrew Mehrtens, Frank Bunce and Walter Little (twice). Gavin Hastings was once again the star of the show for Scotland, kicking 15 points in his final Test, while Doddie Weir got a brace of tries and Scott Hastings the other.

Pool matches:
Scotland 89 Ivory Coast 0
Scotland 41 Tonga 5
Scotland 19 France 22

Quarter-final:
Scotland 30 New Zealand 48

— LAP DANCING ACCIES —

For once the prize for the most adventurous sponsorship deal by a Scottish rugby club doesn't go to a curry house. Glasgow Accies caused a storm when they were sponsored by lap dancing club.

— SCOTLAND LEGENDS XV: IAN McLAUCHLAN —

A member of Scotland's Mean Machine in the early 1970s, the deeply abrasive loose-head from deepest Ayrshire was one of the game's great scrummagers despite standing at just 5ft 10in and weighing in at an anorexic 13 stone 10lbs. A self-assured hardman who was also a ferocious competitor (he played in the 1973 Calcutta Cup two weeks after breaking a bone in his leg), McLauchlan provided a hard edge to whatever team he was playing for and as captain of his country turned Murrayfield into a fortress where Scotland lost only once under his leadership.

For a player whose career was so storied, McLauchlan was a late starter who didn't win his first cap until he was 26. Yet from that 1969 Calcutta Cup to the moment he hung up his boots after the home defeat to Graham Mourie's All Blacks 11 seasons later, his was a career with a relentlessly upwards trajectory.

Unlike his long-term partner in crime Gordon Brown, who made his debut the game after McLauchlan but was only at his best with the Lions, McLauchlan excelled whether he was playing for his country or the world's most famous touring team. However, like Tom Smith after him, it was performing for the Lions which cemented his reputation as one of the best players of his generation.

McLauchlan was one of just five players and the only Scot to play in all eight Tests of the 1971 and 1974 Lions tours, but he was actually lucky to be selected in 1971 and was only included by Carwyn James at the last minute. But once there, he got his chance when Sandy Carmichael was savaged in Christchurch. He took that chance with both hands, capping a storming opening Test with the winning chargedown try in Dunedin (like Brown, he never scored for Scotland). It was his destructive scrummaging against far bigger opponents and his dynamism in the loose that led fellow Scot and tour manager Doug Smith to give him the moniker 'Mighty Mouse'. In South Africa in 1974 he was at his abrasive best, unfeasibly mobile in the loose, destructive in the tight and always ready for a rammy should the need arise, as it often did.

Yet in many ways McLauchlan's most impressive feats came when he was playing for Scotland, and in particular during the record 19 occasions when he captained his country (of which ten were wins). Understated but with damaging intent, McLauchlan led from the front and his sides followed; no-one enjoyed travelling to Murrayfield in the late 1970s. With his long-term club and college mentor Bill Dickinson now Scotland coach (Dickinson was a scrummaging expert who had persuaded the prop to lift weights and study the technique of the dark art) McLauchlan's personality was infused into the team: cussed, aggressive and painfully hard to beat.

Ian McLauchlan vital statistics
Caps: 43 (1969–79)
Position: Loose-head prop
Club: Jordanhill

— KEEP TRYING —

Players who've gone the longest without scoring a try for Scotland:

- Alan Tait made his Scotland debut at the 1987 Rugby World Cup and scored four tries in his four matches in the tournament. The following year he switched to Rugby League and spent eight successful seasons with Widnes and Leeds before returning to Union with Newcastle in 1996. He was reintroduced into the Scotland side against Ireland on 1st March 1997 and scored a try in the 38–10 win – nine years, eight months and 23 days after his last try for Scotland!
- Alex Angus was first capped in 1909 and scored two tries in 14 matches before the First World War. He won four more caps in 1920, scoring a try in the 19–0 win against Ireland on 28th February, nine years and four days after his previous international try.
- Gary Armstrong scored five tries in an outstanding international career which spanned ten years and 51 caps. He scored four tries in his first 21 internationals, his fourth being against Ireland in the 1991 Rugby World Cup at Murrayfield on 12th October. His fifth and final try came almost eight years to the day later against Uruguay in the 1999 Rugby World Cup, also at Murrayfield, on 8th October.

— FIRST REPLACEMENT —

Scrum-half Ian McCrae was Scotland's first replacement when he came on for Gordon Connell against France at Stade Colombes on 11th January 1969. He was involved in the build-up to Jim Telfer's famous match-winning try.

— CLUB AND COUNTRY TEAM-MATES —

Edinburgh have contributed a record nine players to the Scotland starting XV on three occasions:

Scotland 20 France 16, Murrayfield, 5th February 2006
Hugo Southwell, Chris Paterson, Marcus Di Rollo, Mike Blair, Dougie Hall, Alistair Kellock, Scott Murray, Simon Taylor and Allister Hogg

South Africa 29 Scotland 15, Port Elizabeth, 17th June 2006
Southwell, Paterson, Di Rollo, Simon Webster, Blair, Hall, Craig Smith, Kellock and Hogg

Scotland 21 Wales 9, Murrayfield, 10th February 2007
Southwell, Di Rollo, Rob Dewey, Paterson, Godman, Hall, Murray, Taylor and David Callam

— YOUNG GUNS —

The youngest players to be capped by Scotland are:

- **Ninian Finlay** was aged 17 years and 36 days when he was capped out of Edinburgh Academy v England on 8th March 1875.
- **Charles Reid** was aged 17 years and 36 days when he was capped out of Edinburgh Academy v Ireland on 19th February 1881.

Of this pair, Finlay is generally accepted as the youngest to play for Scotland as Reid lived through an extra leap year day!

Remarkably, when Reid won his second cap against England, Frank Wright, one of his classmates at Edinburgh Academy, was called up as a late replacement for England. The only occasion when two schoolboys, let alone classmates, have been capped in opposition.

The following were also capped as schoolboys for Scotland:

Willie Neilson (Merchiston Castle) age 17 years 5 months in 1891
Gordon Neilson (Merchiston Castle) age 17 years 5 months in 1891 (he replaced injured brother George against England to make his debut alongside brother Willie)
D.M. Grant (Elstow) age circa 18 years in 1911
Marshall Reid (Loretto) age 18 years 5 months in 1883
Thomas Anderson (Merchiston Castle) age 18 years 9 months in 1882
James Campbell (Merchiston Castle) age circa 20 years in 1878
William Grant (Craigmount) age circa 20 years in 1873

— FIRST BORN —

According to confirmed records Angus Buchanan (Royal High School FP) is the first Scotland player born – on 15th January 1847. Buchanan is also famous for scoring the first try in international rugby and was 24 years and two months when capped.

However R. Munro (St Andrews University), who also played in the first international against England in 1871, may well have been born in 1839 although there is no firm proof of this. If so, he would have been around the age of 31 at the time of his cap which would have been very old for the time. The average age of the Scotland team for the first match was just over 22.

— TRANSFORMATIONS —

The biggest deficit Scotland have overturned to win a match was against France at Murrayfield on 16th February 1980. Scotland trailed 4–14 midway through the second half but rallied to win 22–14 mainly thanks to the brilliance of Andy Irvine who scored two tries and 16 of Scotland's 18 points in a devastating 12-minute spell.

The biggest lead Scotland have thrown away was also against France at Murrayfield, this time on 4th February 1979. The Scots had led 13–0 at one stage, courtesy of tries by Dave Shedden and Andy Irvine, and one conversion and one penalty by Dougie Morgan. However, Irvine injured his shoulder scoring his try and went off for treatment. Down to 14 men Scotland quickly conceded a try and the momentum was with France, who scored 16 unanswered points. Morgan's drop goal restored parity but a late French penalty made the final score 19–16 to the visitors.

— NO WINNER —

Scotland have drawn a total of 30 matches, against the following nations:

17 v England
5 v Ireland
3 v Wales
3 v France
2 v New Zealand
1 v Western Samoa

— TEN TRY CLUB —

Players who have scored ten or more tries for Scotland:

Player	Tries	Years played
Ian Smith	24	1924–33
Tony Stanger	24	1989–98
Chris Paterson	21	2000–
Gavin Hastings	17	1986–95
Alan Tait	17	1987–99
Gregor Townsend	17	1993–2002
Iwan Tukalo	15	1985–92
Kenny Logan	13	1992–2003
Arthur Smith	12	1955–62
A.C. 'Johnny' Wallace	11	1923–26
Andy Irvine	10	1972–82

— WE'LL WIN AGAIN ONE DAY —

Scotland lost a record 17 consecutive matches between 13th January 1951 (defeated 14–12 by France at Stade Colombes) and 8th January 1955 (defeated 15–0 by France, again at Stade Colombes).

The depressing sequence also included a 44–0 thumping at home to the touring Springboks on 24th November 1951. Finally, the rot was well and truly stopped dead in its tracks when the Scots defeated Wales 14–8 at Murrayfield with Arthur Smith's brilliant debut try acting as the catalyst. A magnificent wing three-quarter, Smith went on to enjoy an outstanding international career which culminated in him captaining the 1962 Lions to South Africa.

— THE CALCUTTA CUP AFFAIR —

John Jeffrey was pulled out of a Scotland sevens side for the NSW International Sevens in Sydney in 1988 after what became known as the Calcutta Cup affair. Jeffrey and England's Dean Richards pinched the silver cup from its pedestal at Murrayfield and played rugby with it up and down Rose Street. When it was replaced two hours later, the much-dented trophy was clearly the worse for wear, rather like Jeffrey and Richards.

"It will now have to be re-named the Calcutta Shield," quipped an unnamed SRU official.

— 100 UP, 50 DOWN —

Matches where Scotland have scored 100 pts:

Scotland 100 Japan 8 at McDiarmid Park, Perth, 13th November 2004

Matches where Scotland have conceded 50 points or more:

Scotland 15 New Zealand 51, Murrayfield, 20th November 1993
New Zealand 62 Scotland 31, Dunedin, 15th June 1996
Scotland 10 South Africa 68, Murrayfield, 6th December 1997
Scotland 16 France 51, Murrayfield, 21st February 1998
New Zealand 69 Scotland 20, Dunedin, 24th June 2000
France 51 Scotland 9, Sydney, 25th October 2003

— CAPTAIN ON DEBUT —

- **Hon. Francis Moncreiff** v England on 27th March 1871 at Raeburn Place
- **Louis Greig** v New Zealand on 18th November 1905 at Inverleith
- **Keith Geddes** v France on 1st January 1947 at Stade Colombes
- **Doug Keller** v France on 15th January 1949 at Stade Colombes

Geddes led Scotland in the first full international match after the Second World War against France on 1st January 1947 at Stade Colombes. A full back, he opened the scoring with a penalty. With the score still 3–0 in Scotland's favour he was involved in a chase for the ball which went over the Scotland try line. The referee was unsighted and awarded Scotland a 25 yard drop out. But Geddes remonstrated with the referee, insisting that French wing Jacques Lassegue had scored a try. The try was then awarded and France went on to win 8–3.

At the banquet after the match the French players presented Geddes with a silver cigarette case which was inscribed, "To commemorate a magnificent example of fair play". Unfortunately, the SRU's enforcement of the strict amateur rules of the time meant that he could not keep the gift.

— NO WORLD CUP HERE, THANKS —

When a proposal to stage a World Cup was put to the SRU in 1982, the Union's Committee voted unanimously against it, declaring itself to be "totally against the proposal".

— SHORTEST TEST CAREER —

Since replacements were first allowed in 1969, 12 Scotland players have won single caps as replacements:

Bill Macdonald v Ireland in 1969
Steve Turk v England in 1971
Hamish Bryce v Ireland in 1973
Jimmy Gossman v England in 1980
Ian Corcoran v Australia in 1992
Paul Jones v Wales in 1992
Scott Nichol v Argentina in 1994
John Manson v England in 1995
Cameron Glasgow v France in 1997
Andrew Hall v USA in 2002
Andrew Dall v Wales in 2003
Andrew Wilson v Romania in 2005

The players on the pitch for the shortest time are:

- Bill Macdonald, capped v Ireland on 2nd February 1969 at Murrayfield. After replacing Chris Rea with less than five minutes remaining he did not touch the ball or make a tackle.
- Cameron Glasgow, capped v France on 15th March 1997 at Parc des Princes as a 74th minute replacement for Alan Tait.
- Andrew Hall, capped v USA on 22nd June 2002 in San Francisco as a 77th minute replacement for Jason White.

— HALL OF FAME —

There are five Scots in the 55-man International Rugby Hall of Fame: Ian McGeechan (inducted 1995), Andy Irvine (1999), Bill McLaren (2001), Gordon Brown (2001) and Gavin Hastings (2003). The following countries are also represented: New Zealand (12 members), Wales (9), Australia (7), France (6), Ireland (6), South Africa (5), England (3) and Argentina (1).

There are seven rugby players in the Scottish Sports Hall of Fame in Edinburgh: Finlay Calder OBE, Doug Elliot, Gavin Hastings OBE, Andy Irvine MBE, GPS Macpherson CBE, Mark Morrison and Wilson Shaw. Swimming (including diving and water polo) has nine members, while boxing has six.

— NOT SO SMUG AFTERWARDS —

Before the final match of the 2000 Six Nations, a Calcutta Cup clash between England and Scotland at Murrayfield and a match which England needed to win to collect a Grand Slam, England's supporters started taking what they supposed to be their hosts' status as doormats for granted. Spot the difference between some of these before and after assessments of the match:

Before:

"The headlong rush into professionalism has carried England so far ahead of the Celtic nations that we are disappearing over the horizon."
Mick Dennis, *London Evening Standard*, March 2000

"It's in the bag for England. Barring some unforeseen catastrophe, Woodward's men look to have a certain Grand slam today."
The Observer

"Will England be denied as they were in 1990? The odds are firmly against such a notion. No miracle, just a massacre. In the Six Nations showdown at Murrayfield, England to win by 44 points to take the Grand Slam today."
Welshman **Stephen Jones** in *The Sunday Times*

"England or France will put 100 points on a Celtic nation before the end of the century."
Former England lock **Paul Ackford** writing in *The Sunday Telegraph*

"To lose one Grand Slam last year [when Wales beat them in the final minute of the final match to deny them a Grand Slam] was careless; to lose two, all but impossible."
Stephen Jones in *The Sunday Times*

"Can you really see England losing this?"
Scotland-supporting TV journalist **John Inverdale** to his co-commentators before kick-off

After:

"Of all the victories in my career this rates pretty highly, especially after the season we have had."
Scotland coach **Ian McGeechan** after fly-half Duncan Hodge's try sealed a famous 19–13 for Scotland in atrocious conditions.

"It was a breakdown in communications."
RFU President **John Addison** apologises to the spectators and sponsors after England's players ran straight to the dressing-room rather than staying to collect the Six Nations trophy after their 2000 loss at Murrayfield

"Whhhhhhhaaaaayyyhoooooo."
Scotland summariser **Alan Tait**; his co-commentator Jeremy Guscott maintained a steely silence

"I never believed we were going to lose the game and I won't really believe it until I wake up. I am really mad about that."
England coach **Clive Woodward**

"It feels like last year, I can't say any more. We didn't play well, our discipline wasn't great and the penalty count against us was huge."
Woodward again

"I am glad we didn't win the Grand Slam because as coach, I am still hungry to achieve something with this England team."
Woodward tries to put a positive spin on a gut-wrenching experience. He was later to perfect this art as coach of the Lions to New Zealand in 2005.

— MOST CAPPED REF —

Jim Fleming refereed a total of 40 full international matches. He made his international debut in 1985 when he refereed Ireland against England at Lansdowne Road. In addition to these 40 matches with whistle in hand he acted as touch judge another 75 times. Furthermore, he officiated at the first four Rugby World Cups in 1987, 1991, 1995 and 1999, reffing 12 matches.

Other credits to his name include 18 consecutive appearances at the Melrose Sevens and for his final official match he became the first Scotsman to referee Scotland in the modern era when he was in charge for the match against the Barbarians at Murrayfield on 24th May 2001.

— THERE'S ONLY TWO TOM SCOTTS! —

In 1898, two players called Tom Scott turned out for Scotland against Ireland. Both also played for Hawick. That's where the similarities ended: one was a speedy wing who scored two tries that day, the other was a gnarled forward who didn't.

— HAT-TRICK HEROES —

Date	Player	Opposition	Tries	Venue
19th Feb 1877	Robert McKenzie*	Ireland	3	Belfast
21st Feb 1891	Willie Wotherspoon*	Ireland	3	Belfast
26th Feb 1887	George Lindsay	Wales	5	Raeburn Place
22nd Jan 1910	James Tennant	France	3	Inverleith
1st Jan 1913	Willie Stewart*	France	3	Parc des Princes
22nd Feb 1913	Willie Stewart	Ireland	4	Inverleith
2nd Feb 1924	Ian Smith*	Wales	3	Inverleith
24th Jan 1925	Ian Smith	France	4	Inverleith
7th Feb 1925	Ian Smith	Wales	4	Swansea
2nd Jan 1926	AC 'Johnny' Wallace	France	3	Stades Colombes
2nd June 1987	John Jeffrey	Romania	3	Dunedin
4th March 1989	Iwan Tukalo	Ireland	3	Murrayfield
9th Dec 1989	Tony Stanger	Romania	3	Murrayfield
9th Oct 1991	Iwan Tukalo	Zimbabwe	3	Murrayfield
26th May 1995	Gavin Hastings	Ivory Coast	4	Rustenberg
24th Nov 2002	Andy Craig	Fiji	3	Murrayfield
13th Nov 2004	Chris Paterson	Japan	4	Perth

* Debut for Scotland

— DOMINANT ERA —

Hawick won the first official National League Division One title in 1972/73 and went on to win it for five successive seasons: 1972/723, 1973/74, 1974/75, 1975/76 and 1976/77 to completely dominate the Scottish club scene during this period. They have won the League title a record 12 times.

The Greens were also the first winners of the Border League title in 1901/02 and of the inaugural Scottish Cup in 1995/96.

— SMITHY SLAYS ENGLAND —

Ian Smith is Scotland's record try-scorer against England with nine in five matches.

— SCOTTISH SCHOOLS CUP WINNERS —

1983/84: North Berwick High School
1984/85: Galashiels Academy
1985/86: Galashiels Academy
1986/87: Kelso High School
1987/88: Galashiels Academy
1988/89: St Aloysius' College
1989/90: St Aloysius' College
1990/91: Galashiels Academy
1991/92: Marr College
1992/93: St Aloysius' College
1993/94: Marr College
1994/95: St Aloysius' College
1995/96: St Aloysius' College
1996/97: Galashiels Academy
1997/98: Merchiston Castle School
1998/99: Stewart's Melville College
1999/00: Merchiston Castle School
2000/01: Merchiston Castle School
2000/02: Merchiston Castle School
2002/03: Dollar Academy
2003/04: Dollar Academy
2004/05: Dollar Academy
2005/06: Stewart's Melville College
2006/07: Bell Baxter High School

— WOODEN SPOON —

Scotland have won the Wooden Spoon 23 times, in the following years:

1902*, 1911*, 1928, 1930, 1932*, 1935, 1936*, 1939, 1947*, 1952*, 1953*, 1954*, 1956, 1959, 1965, 1968*, 1971, 1978*, 1979, 1985, 1994, 2004*, 2007

* Whitewash

— BOOT BOOB —

When England travelled to Glasgow to play Scotland in 1873, the conditions were so wet that the visitors sent their boots off to the cobbler to have steel bars inserted in them (to act like studs). However, several of the boots got lost and C.W. Boyle, one of England's speediest backs, ended up playing with one boot and one dress shoe.

— SCOTLAND'S GREATEST GAMES 6 —

Scotland 19 Wales 0
Murrayfield
3rd February 1951

The circumstances of this Scottish win were absolutely remarkable. With 15 internationals killed during the war and countless future Test players doubtless missing too, Scotland's fortunes took a nosedive in the post-war era. Before this match they had lost 12 of their 18 international matches since the war, and after this match they would not win another until 1955, a run of 17 consecutive defeats which included the horror-show 44–0 home defeat by the Springboks.

So confident were the Welsh that they travelled north with 20,000 spectators, who helped swell the crowd to a record 80,000. And they had every reason to be smug: Wales had won the Grand Slam the year before and had a team of all the talents which included 11 1950 Lions; while Scotland had a young team that had won just two of its last seven matches. Scotland had not beaten Wales since 1938 and there were few reasons to think that was about to change.

Wales certainly started brightly, and began to press the Scottish defences, but as the game wore on the home forwards began to take the game to the men in red and gradually the majority of the play began to take place in the Welsh 25. The balance of play in the first half was accurately reflected by a 3–0 lead at the interval after debutant Heriot's fullback I.H.M. Thomson, who had only been called into the side that morning, landed a sweetly-struck penalty.

If the first half was nip and tuck, the second was all Scotland. It was all Wales could do to hold on, with Gordon, Elliot and Rose all going close. Then the dam broke when full back Williams put in a hurried clearance that landed in Scotland skipper Peter Kininmonth's hands, whereupon the big No.8 simply looked up and casually stroked over a perfect drop goal from the touchline. From the moment that the most famous drop goal in Scottish rugby history flew between the posts it was all one-way traffic. Scotland ran in three late tries, with Gordon grabbing a brace and Dawson getting the other, the last two of which resulted from traditional dribbling runs from the Scottish forwards.

They may not have tasted the joy of victory again for another four years (they beat Wales four years and two days later with another equally unexpected, if slightly less emphatic, Murrayfield victory) but at least this time three-quarters of rugby's record attendance left with a smile on their faces.

— WIND-UP PAYS DIVIDENDS —

In 1990, shortly before the Grand Slam game against England, several of the senior players got together and decided that what they needed was a distraction to take everyone's minds off the game. What they came up with was a wind-up of monumental proportions, with John Jeffrey as the dupe.

It started a couple of days before the game when Jeffrey and Fin Calder were with a group of players at an Edinburgh pub. All of a sudden a pretty blonde rushed in and called Calder to one side, saying to him: "Fin, the test is positive, we must talk," before tearfully leaving the pub pursued by Calder, a happily married man with two children. The rest of the players surveyed the scene in shocked silence. Jeffrey worried for his friend and fretted over the situation all night.

On the bus the next day a letter was handed to the bus driver marked for Calder's attention. When someone said it looked like women's writing, Sean Lineen grabbed it, opened it and started to read out the letter, in which the woman begged Calder to do the right thing by her. By this stage Jeffrey was desperately trying to get through the throng of players to physically restrain Lineen, but just as the White Shark battled to within feet of the Kiwi, the centre read out the postscript: "J.J., you've been had".

As a way of breaking the tension the joke was perfect, bonding the squad together in readiness for the showdown with the Auld Enemy.

England, meanwhile, were engaging in the same sort of group bonding session, but with slightly different results. John Olver, the squad hooker and an enthusiastic countryman, had arranged for the England squad to go pheasant shooting on an estate outside Edinburgh. Several of the squad had never been let loose with a firearm before and were quite nervous, but it was Olver who disgraced himself by shooting at a bird before checking where all of his fellow guns had gone.

Unfortunately for him, No.8 Mike Teague had gone for a wander and was right in the line of fire, going down like a sack of spuds. The next thing Teague remembers is coming too with a sore throbbing pain in his backside and Dean Richards, Teague's rival for the No.8 spot, leaning over him, shouting: "Is he dead? Have you killed the bugger? Do you think he'll be able to play?"

Teague left an indecent pause before opening one eye and saying, "Of course I'll be able to play. Now go and get the tweezers – someone seems to have shot me in the arse and I want you to remove the pellets." He didn't see Richards for dust . . .

— SCOTLAND LEGENDS XV: ANDY IRVINE —

The Swashbuckling Andy Irvine

When the SRU ran a poll for the best attacking player to have played for Scotland, the swashbuckling Andy Irvine won by a country mile. A thrilling runner and counter-attacker, the Heriot's full back had pace, verve and daring by the bucketload and for 11 seasons he was a shining beacon for those who longed to see intuitive, edge-of-the-seat rugby played at speed.

It didn't always work, and Irvine had detractors who pointed to his supposed frailty under the high ball and the defensive weaknesses that saw him start his international career on the wing. But Irvine's attitude was that it was better to have run and lost than never to have run, and by and large his great talent saw to it that he shocked his opponents rather than his own supporters.

One match encapsulates the enigma that was Irvine. In 1980, playing the French at Murrayfield, things were going so badly that he was being relentlessly booed following a missed penalty from in front of the posts. Then, with less than ten minutes remaining, he ghosted in for two exhilarating solo scores, plus a conversion and two penalties, to turn 14–4 down into a 22–14 victory which brought the house down. It was a devastating match-winning cameo that French sports newspaper *L'Equipe* rewarded by temporarily renaming the stadium 'Irvinefield'.

As with Brown and McLauchlan, Irvine was also part of the generation of British players in the 1970s who went down to the Southern Hemisphere and set new standards with the Lions. Although the presence of the defensively impeccable J.P.R. Williams meant that Irvine was moved to the wing in the first of his three Lions tours in 1974, he still managed to be the star of the show, running in five tries against King Country-Manawatu and scoring a record 156 points in 1974.

His Scotland stats aren't too shabby either: in 51 appearances he scored ten tries and 261 points, and captained his country 15 times.

Andy Irvine vital statistics
Caps: 51 (1972–82)
Position: Full back
Club: Heriot's FP

— RFU MEMBERSHIP —

Almost as soon as it was formed, the RFU was joined by several Scottish clubs. Glasgow Academical, West of Scotland and Edinburgh University joined in 1871 and Edinburgh Academicals and Royal HSFP joined in 1872. All five left when the SFU (the forerunner of the SRU) was set up shortly afterwards. London Scottish, however, remain members of both the SRU and RFU.

— WRIGHT ON TRACK —

Frank Wright, born in Leigh but living in Glasgow, won his only cap for England against Scotland on 19th March 1881 because half-back Henry Taylor of Blackheath missed the train to Edinburgh.

— BILL McLAREN IN QUOTES —

The legendary Bill McLaren

"A day out of Hawick is a day wasted"

"That could have made it 10–3 and there's a subtle difference between that and 7–3."

"His sidestep was marvellous – like a shaft of lightning."
On Gerald Davies

"I look at Colin Meads and see a great big sheep farmer who carried the ball in his hands as though it was an orange pip."
On All Blacks legend Colin Meads

"The Scottish midfield opened up like the Gobi desert."

"He's like a buffalo leading a stampede."
On Scott Gibbs' Grand Slam-denying try against England at Wembley in 1999

"Now he can run – but not if he hasn't got any legs."
As Austin Healy was tackled on his own five-metre line in that same 1999 game

"To see a Borders rugby game is to witness the intensity, fervour, rivalry and spirit of the Scottish Borders."

— WOODY AND IDS —

Sir Clive Woodward, the man who led England to World Cup success in 2003 and who chose as few Scots as possible when he led the Lions to New Zealand on the ill-fated 2006 tour, went to school in Portobello, in Edinburgh, where he developed a love for the round ball game. This so disturbed his father that he sent him to the rugby-only boarding school HMS Conway, where he soon showed his talent playing as a fly-half outside a small but combative scum-half called Iain Duncan-Smith.

— PASSING THE CHUCK —

Edinburgh University student John Macfarlane, an 1871 'original' who was to die in 1874 from an infection picked up after he dislocated his knee playing rugby, pioneered the practice of passing the ball before being tackled, a development which was referred to as 'chucking'. Before then, all players ploughed on as far as they could before finally releasing the ball or having it ripped from their grasp. It was to become one of the most significant technical innovations the game was ever to see.

— ECLIPSE DRAWS THE CROWD —

Scotland's last match at Inverleith took place on 24th January 1924 against France. The crowd was over 20,000 strong – partly because there was scheduled to be a total eclipse of the sun halfway through the game.

— TOP CAPS —

Scotland's most capped players are:

Player	Caps
Scott Murray (1997–2007)	84
Gregor Townsend (1993–2003)	82
Gordon Bulloch (1997–2005)	75
Chris Paterson (1999–2007)	74
Stuart Grimes (1997–2005)	71
Kenny Logan(1992–2003)	70

— FIRST RADIO AND TV BROADCASTS —

The first live radio broadcast of a rugby match took place in 1927 at Murrayfield when Scotland won the Calcutta Cup 21–13, running in four tries to England's one. Scotland were also involved in the first match to be broadcast live on television: the 1938 Calcutta Cup at Twickenham, which was a showdown for the Triple Crown played in front of 70,000 people.

— MISERY MAKERS —

The players to have scored the most points in total against Scotland:

Andrew Mehrtens (**New Zealand**): 108 points in seven Tests, 1995–2001

Diego Dominguez (**Italy**): 94 points in six Tests,1996–2002

Percy Montgomery (**South Africa**): 89 points in six Tests, 1997–2006

Neil Jenkins (**Wales**): 88 points in nine Tests, 1991–2001

David Humphreys (**Ireland**): 84 points in ten Tests, 1997–2005

Jonny Wilkinson (**England**): 82 points in six Tests, 1999–2007

Matt Burke (**Australia**): 79 points in five Tests, 1996–2004

Paul Grayson (**England**): 75 points in five Tests, 1995–2004

Ronan O'Gara (**Ireland**): 71 points in seven Tests, 2000–2007

Grant Fox (**New Zealand**): 54 points in three Tests, 1987–1990

— LESLIE BALFOUR —

Leslie Balfour was arguably the most remarkable sportsman ever to pull on a Scotland jersey in any sport. An Edinburgh Academical, he was picked to play in the first international in 1871 while still 16, and would still be comfortably the youngest player ever to have played for Scotland had he taken the field. However, days before the match he received a nasty bite from a stray dog and had to pull out of the match. He made his Scotland debut the next year, still a month shy of his 18th birthday, but that was to be his only cap.

Rugby aside, Balfour had an impressive pedigree across the whole sporting spectrum. He would almost certainly have won many more caps for Scotland had he spent more time playing rugby, but his other sporting interests – not to mention his career as a high-flying lawyer who eventually became Writer to the Signet – made that impossible. As well as winning the Scottish Lawn Tennis Championship in 1879, Balfour was also the Scottish billiards champion and represented his country at skating, curling, athletics and the long jump.

But all that was peanuts compared to Balfour's achievements in his two greatest sporting loves: golf and cricket. In an era where many of the best golfers were still amateurs, Balfour excelled at Scotland's national game, winning the Amateur Championship at St Andrews in 1895 and being the runner-up in 1889. Indeed, in the ten years between 1888 and 1897, as well as reaching those two finals he made it to six semi-finals. When he won the Championship in 1895, he did so by beating John Ball – the reigning Open champion, four-time Amateur champion and the first golfer to hold the Open and Amateur titles at the same time – by one hole.

Yet, if anything, Balfour's fame as a cricketer was even greater than his renown as a golfer. Known as 'the W.G. Grace of Scotland', he was first picked to represent Scotland against England while still 15 years old. As well as making 46 centuries in a long career that ended in his seventies (he won his last cap for Scotland aged 55), he captained Scotland to victory over Australia at the Grange in 1882 in a result that remains arguably the biggest upset in the history of the sport. As captain, wicket-keeper and opening batsman, Balfour's flowing innings of 73 was largely responsible for defeating an Australian side that had already beaten Scotland by an innings and which would go on to humiliate England in the match which would bring the Ashes into being.

As well as being a remarkable all-rounder, he also proved to be an inspired administrator who was president of the SRU, president of the Scottish Cricket Union and the captain of the Royal and Ancient Golf

Club at St Andrews. His son also played cricket for Scotland before being killed in the First World War. Balfour changed his name to Balfour-Melville in 1893 when his father succeeded to the estate of Mount Melville near St Andrews (at which stage his name became Leslie Melville Balfour-Melville – so good they named him twice, as one wag noted).

— SEVENS FIRSTS —

The first non-Scottish club to win one of the Borders sevens titles was Tynedale, who won the Gala Sevens in 1885. The first sevens tournament to take place outside Scotland was the Percy Park Sevens in North Shields in 1921, although the final was contested between winners Selkirk and runners-up Melrose. The biggest tournament south of the border, the Middlesex Sevens, first took place at Twickenham on 24th April 1926 and was set up and organised by Dr J.A. Russell-Cargill, a London-based Scot.

— ISLE OF BUTE ALL BLACK —

Jack Manchester's All Black tourists of 1935/36 beat Scotland 18–8 thanks in part to three conversions from full back Mike Gilbert, who had been born in Rothesay on the Isle of Bute before emigrating to New Zealand. Gilbert played in 27 of the 30 matches on tour and was the top scorer with 125 points.

— FAMILY CONNECTIONS —

There are two families in which grandfather and father had played Union for Scotland before the son represented the country at League. Chris Simmers, who played for Scotland's RL side in 1996, was the son of Brian Simmers (seven Union caps 1965–71); and grandson of Max Simmers (28 Union caps 1926–32), while Struan Douglas, who represented Scotland twice at League in 1995, was the son of John Douglas (12 Union caps 1961–63 and a British Lion) and grandson of Alec Brown (three Union caps 1928–29).

— SCOTLAND LEGENDS XV: JOHN RUTHERFORD —

John Rutherford: the best playmaker ever to wear the thistle

'Rud' may not have won as many caps as Gregor Townsend or Craig Chalmers, nor played as many times for the Lions, but he was a blueblood among fly-halves, a languid player with a beautiful economy of movement and the ability to absolutely dominate the hurly-burly of international rugby.

What's more, the Selkirk stand-off wasn't just naturally talented; even after he made his international debut against Wales in 1979 he worked incredibly hard to turn himself into the complete player. In particular, he worked so hard on his cover tackling that he almost became an auxiliary flanker, while his hours spent practising drop-kicks at Philliphaugh paid dividends, with his 12 drop goals for Scotland still a record. He also worked hard on his kicking, but while he morphed from a primarily running No.10 to one who could kick the ball prodigious distances, he never became a kicking fly-half, just one who could adapt to any conditions and was happy to play whatever game was most likely to bring a win.

For much of his career with Scotland, Rutherford struck up a highly profitable partnership with scrum-half Roy Laidlaw, a fellow Borderer more in the traditional mould of a terrier-like half-back capable of sniping around the base of the scrum and breakdown. An astute player, the nuggety Laidlaw gave Rutherford the time to work his magic, and the Selkirk maestro took full advantage, making himself the fulcrum around which the 1984 Grand Slam-winning side revolved. The two played together a record 35 times, and on the eight occasions between 1980–87 when they didn't play together, Scotland lost seven.

Despite taking centre stage at a time when Scotland were a formidable force – he masterminded the 33–6 humiliation of England at Twickenham, for instance, and it was generally held that when he played well, so did Scotland – Rutherford only made one appearance for the Lions, which came on the 1983 tour to New Zealand when he scored a try from centre while playing outside Ollie Campbell. By the time the 1989 Lions tour came into view, Rutherford had retired. He also missed the 1987 World Cup when he took an unauthorised trip to a fun tournament in Bermuda and damaged his leg, an injury which gave out five minutes into the first game of the inaugural World Cup. It was an irony lost on no-one because since he had made his debut Rutherford had sustained no serious injuries and had played in every Scotland international over the previous eight years.

Not that any of that can dim the memory of a player who deserves to be remembered as the best playmaker ever to wear the thistle.

John Rutherford vital statistics
Caps: 42 (1979–87)
Position: Fly-half
Club: Selkirk

— SCOTLAND DON'T TURN UP —

Scotland cancelled their Five Nations trip to Dublin in 1972 at the height of 'The Troubles' amid heightened security fears of a possible attack by the IRA. England went, although they were beaten 16–12, prompting skipper Peter Wheeler's famous quip at the post-match dinner: "We may be rubbish, but at least we turn up."

— ONE BROWN IN, ANOTHER OUT —

Gordon Brown made his debut in 1969 in the famous 6–3 win over the touring Springboks. His second cap, won in the first match of the next year's Five Nations, didn't go too well, though, with Pierre Villepreux playing a blinder and the French winning 11–9 at Murrayfield.

In those days the selectors tended to have a more knee-jerk approach to picking the side, so 'Broon fae Troon' went to work in his local bank and waited nervously for the news of the team to play Wales in Cardiff. Just before lunch, the bank's manager sent a message down to him: there was an urgent call from his brother about the team to play Wales.

Brown dashed over to the phone and asked his brother Peter (known to all and sundry as 'PC') what was going in. "I'm in!" screamed PC in obvious delight.

"That's brilliant!" shouted Gordon. "So who's out?"

"You are," laughed his brother.

The story has a happy ending, though: Gordon came on as a replacement when his brother limped off just after half-time in Cardiff, although Scotland were soundly beaten, losing 18–9.

— C'EST IMPOSSIBLE! —

The editor of French rugby paper *Midi L'Olympique*, Richard Lescot, is one of the most respected journalists in world rugby and a colossus of rugby writing in France. His rugby hero was 1987 European Player of the Year John Rutherford. Lescot had never had the chance to visit the ground where the Scot honed his skills and so when Rutherford retired from international rugby after the first World Cup, the Frenchman made the journey to Selkirk to visit Philliphaugh, the ground where Rutherford played his club rugby.

When he first clapped eyes on the rutted ground with its tiny main (only) stand he refused to believe this was the nursery that had nurtured Rutherford's genius and was convinced that his workmates had played an elaborate practical joke on him. Only when his taxi driver had driven him around town several times in a vain attempt to find the 'real' ground did he finally accept that there was no wind-up in progress.

— NICHOL'S LATE CALL UP —

Veteran Scotland scrum-half Andy Nicol was leading a group of rugby tourists in Australia in 2001 when he was called into the Lions party at short notice. He came off the bench in the third and deciding Test, which Australia won 29–23. Nicol, Bath's captain when they won the Heineken Cup in 1998, was one of Scotland's two representatives in the World XV which played the All Blacks in 1992. Gavin Hastings was the other.

— SCOTLAND'S GREATEST GAMES 7 —

England 6 Scotland 33
Twickenham
18th January 1986

Of all Scotland's 41 Calcutta Cup victories, none have been achieved with as much poise and panache as the 1986 win over an England side which had already beaten Ireland and Wales by the time the two teams met at Twickenham. Despite the list of big names on the England teamsheet – Dooley, Winterbottom, Halliday, Salmon, Andrew, Melville, Rendall and Colclough et al – Scotland blew them away in a second half of stunning intensity in which the English were little more than bystanders. Scotland scored three tries after the interval, but it could easily have been double that.

There was no hint of the carnage to come during the first half even though Gavin Hastings had kicked Scotland into a 12–6 half-time lead. But once the interval was out of the way, the visitors unleashed controlled havoc as they picked apart England's threadbare defences. The destroyer-in-chief was stand-off John Rutherford, who put in one of the stand-out performances of a stellar career. Indeed, his second-half try remains one of the best Calcutta Cup scores of all time, as he first veered left and then sidestepped right, leaving three would-be tacklers "dangling like puppets on a string" as one eminent reporter put it.

Not that Matt Duncan's explosion of pace for his try in the corner or Scott Hastings' subtle handling skills for his late touchdown, which was converted by his brother, were too shabby. In fact, rarely have Scotland managed to put together a half of such incisive quality.

— FROM UNION TO LEAGUE —

The ranks of Scottish rugby have never been heavily depleted by incursions from Rugby League scouts. This was partly because so many of the early greats came from the FP clubs whose members would have frowned on the idea of professional sport, and partly because of a rare instance of SRU prescience that led to the setting up of the Borders League. This, in turn, stymied the growing links between the mill towns of the Borders and their counterparts in Yorkshire, where there had been a large-scale move to the professional code.

Nevertheless, more players than is commonly realised have made the great leap between the codes. Virtually all came from the Borders teams, with many leaving the sport before they had won caps. There were, however, enough capped players who took the League shilling in the game's 'closed' era to form a whole international side. Indeed, 15 Scots have gone on to play for the Great Britain League side.

The first Scotland cap to go was Hawick stonemason Alex Laidlaw, one of the first Borderers to be capped, who won his solitary cap against Ireland in 1897 before signing for Bradford the following year. With the sole exception of Heriot's FP and British Lions No.8 Roy Kinnear (the father of the famous actor of the same name who met his death falling off a horse while filming *The Return of the Musketeers* in 1989), all who followed him were fellow Borderers:

Player RU club	Caps	RL move	
Alex Laidlaw	Hawick	1 (1897)	Bradford (1899)
Anthony Little	Hawick	1 (1905)	Wigan (1905/06)
George Douglas	Jedforest	1 (1921)	Batley (1921/22)
Roy Kinnear	Heriot's FP	3 (1926)	Wigan (1926/27)
William Welsh	Hawick	21 (1927–33)	London Highfield 1933/34)
Gordon Cottington	Kelso	5 (1934–36)	Castleford (1936/37)
Gordon Gray	Gala	4 (1935–37)	Huddersfield (1937/38)
Dave Valentine	Hawick	2 (1947)	Huddersfield (1947/48)
Thomas Wright	Hawick	1 (1947)	Leeds (1948/49)
George Wilson	Oxford Univ/ Hawick	3 (1949)	Workington (1950)
David Rose	Jedforest	7 (1951–53)	Huddersfield (1953/54)

Rob Valentine	Hawick	3 (1953)	Huddersfield (1963)
Hugh Duffy	Jedforest	1 (1955)	Salford (1954/55)
Brian Shillinglaw	Gala	5 (1960–61)	Whitehaven (1961/62)
Ron Cowan	Selkirk	5 (1961–62)	Leeds (1962/63)

Since the demise of amateurism in 1995, several high-profile Scotland players have also followed the players listed above. Most notable of these was Kelso's Alan Tait, who had already been capped for Scotland at Union when he left for Widnes, going on to be capped for GB (though selected for the England RL side he refused to play) before playing for Scotland and the British Lions with some distinction on his return from League.

Uncapped Stirling County prop George Graham was another who tried his hand at League before coming back into the fold by joining Newcastle, from where he won 25 caps.

Three of the other four players of note who went to League after 1995 were Anglos: uncapped centre Gareth Morton, centre Andy Craig (23 caps) and wing Jon Steel (five caps). The other, Aussie-born centre Jim McLaren (30 caps), had come from League before returning there in his native Australia.

— BACK ROW RECORD —

Back row trio John Jeffrey, Finlay Calder and Derek White played together 17 times until they retired following the 1991 World Cup, which remains a record.

— WINNING BET —

As part of ITV's 1991 Word Cup commentary team, Gordon Brown once donned cricket whites and tied hankies to his wrists and ankles (in Morris-dancing style) live on air to win a bet.

— FAMILIAR FOE —

Opposition players who have played the most Tests against Scotland:

Mike Gibson (Ireland): 14 Tests (1963–1979)
Jason Leonard (England): 14 tests, 1990–2003

— SCOTLAND AT THE WORLD CUP: 1999, WALES PLUS THE FIVE NATIONS —

Scotland played all of their pool matches at home but somehow, despite their status as reigning Five Nations champions, the tournament failed to catch the imagination of the Scottish public and the matches played north of the border were characterised by some embarrassingly small crowds, including the 6,000 that saw South Africa play Spain. Scotland's campaign was hamstrung from the start when they were beaten 46–29 by the Springboks, a defeat that meant they would finish second in the group despite easy wins over Spain and Uruguay.

A low-key tournament sparked into life as Scotland took on the Samoa side which had dismantled Wales the week before, but ran out comfortable 35–20 winners. Scotland were to go out – yet again – to New Zealand in the quarter-finals, but this time it was a better performance than anyone had expected them to put in. As with that year's Calcutta Cup, however, Scotland started tentatively, giving their illustrious opponents too much respect, before snapping out of it and dominating the second half both territorially and in terms of points. It was too little too late, though, and despite tries from Cammie Murray and Budge Pountney, a golden chance to register a first win over the All Blacks was lost.

Pool matches:
Scotland 29 South Africa 46
Scotland 43 Uruguay 12
Scotland 48 Spain 0

Quarter-final play-off:
Scotland 35 Samoa 20

Quarter-final:
Scotland 18 New Zealand 30

— RUGBY LEAGUE AMATEURS —

There are six amateur Rugby League sides in Scotland: the Easterhouse Panthers, Paisley Hurricanes, Edinburgh Eagles, Moray Eels, Glasgow Bulls and the Fife Lions. At the end of the 2006/07 season, Fife had won the title for three of the last four years, with the Royal Scots Steelers beating them in the only final they lost. Their main challengers continue to be Edinburgh Eagles, a side built around the strong Napier University set-up.

— THE SHOW MUST GO ON —

With the possible exception of South Africa's 1995 World Cup semi-final win over France in Durban, the worst conditions that any match has ever been played in occurred when Scotland met New Zealand in 1975. The tour was due to climax with a one-off Test at Eden Park in Auckland before the tourists flew out the next day, but the night before the Test it started to rain. And it rained . . . and rained . . . and rained. By the next day, more than four inches of rain had fallen and there were huge areas of standing water.

Normally the match would have been cancelled but not only were Scotland flying out, but 53,000 spectators had paid almost £100,000 to watch the match, so the show had to go on. A farce of a game was dominated by the All Blacks and in particular moustachioed scrum-half Sid Going's tactic of launching huge garryowens which rained down from the heavens on the Scotland back three. Indeed, Going's first act was to land one of these bombs on debutant full back Jim Hay – it arrived with three tacklers, one of whom broke the Boroughmuir man's arm with a blatant kick, sending him back to the dressing room after less than five minutes of the game.

The final score was 24–0, all watched by a crowd of 45,000 enthusiastic Kiwis.

— LOST SCOTS —

England and British Lions full back-cum-wing Jason Robinson is just one of the many international players who could have played for Scotland, as the former Rugby League legend's mother was from north of the border. So, too, current All Blacks centre Luke McAlister, whose man-mountain father Charlie won three caps for Scotland at Rugby League.

— ROWING'S GAIN IS RUGBY'S LOSS —

Olympic rowing gold medallist Sir Matthew Pinsent is a Scot from Kelso who was also a very keen rugby player. On his arrival at Oxford University after boarding at Eton, he was told in no uncertain terms that he had to give up his dream of playing in the Varsity Match and also taking part in the Boat Race, and had to choose between the two. He opted for rowing, and a potentially outstanding partnership with Scott Murray went down in history as one of the great 'what-ifs'.

— SCOTLAND LEGENDS XV: COLIN DEANS —

Colin Deans: ferociously focused

Colin Deans' first brush with the beautiful game came at the age of 11 when he went to his school in Hawick and came under the wing of television commentator Bill McLaren, then a teacher. McLaren had played with his father Peter, a tough hooker, at Hawick, and said to the young lad: "You'll be a hooker then!", a prediction which became the title of his autobiography.

Deans *was* a hooker, and a remarkably good one, going on to make his debut for Scotland against France in 1978, barely ten years after first meeting McLaren, and ultimately winning a half-century of caps before retiring a decade later after the 1987 World Cup.

In between, the blisteringly quick and ferociously focused Deans worked so hard on the areas of the game that he could improve – he particularly concentrated on his throwing-in after Derrick Grant suggested he should allow the wings to throw in for him – that he was able to make up for his comparative lack of size and emerge as Scotland's greatest ever hooker.

Deans was a fleet-footed prototype of the modern hooker who played more like a flanker and as such he achieved so much with Scotland, including winning the 1984 Grand Slam, captaining his country 15 times, and leading the Scots into the first World Cup. So it seems wrong for him to be remembered as much for the low point of his career as for its highs.

The low point occurred in 1983, when the Lions' Irish-dominated management named their hooker Ciaran Fitzgerald as the tour captain, dooming Deans to share the fate of John Rutherford and spend the Tests collecting splinters while a palpably inferior player played in the side that was well beaten by the All Blacks.

Colin Deans vital statistics
Caps: 52 (1978–87)
Position: Hooker
Club: Hawick

— EARLY SCORING SYSTEM —

In the early years of international rugby, it was Scotland that pushed for the introduction of a universal points system, but it wasn't until 1891 that the International Board introduced a scoring system that was accepted by all four Home Unions. A try was worth one point, a conversion two points, a drop goal three points, a penalty goal two points and a goal mark three points.

— FAMILIAR FINISH —

Scotland's final game in the World Cup has been against New Zealand in the tournaments of 1987, 1991, 1995 and 1999. The only time the Scots have finished the tournament not being beaten by the All Blacks was in 2003, when they were beaten in the quarter-finals by hosts Australia.

— LAST FOUR-POINTER —

Heart and Sole: Scotland's record-breaking captain

In his final appearance for Scotland, Grand Slam skipper David Sole scored the last try to be worth four points when he barrelled through the Wallaby defence as Scotland were beaten 37–13 at Ballymore in Brisbane in 1992. That game marked the 24th occasion on which he captained Scotland, a record.

— BROTHERS ON DEBUT —

Only two sets of brothers have made their debuts in the same game. In 1891, 17-year-old schoolboy Willie Neilson and his older brother George played their first international game together as Scotland beat Wales 15–0 at Raeburn Place. One of the four Neilson brothers (Gordon, George, Willie and Robert) played for Scotland in each of the 25 matches between the day when Willie and George made their debuts together in 1891 until Robert had to withdraw from the 1899 Calcutta Cup line-up after fracturing his nose.

Almost a century later, Watsonians three-quarters Scott and Gavin Hastings both took their opening bow against France, playing in the 18–17 win in 1986. After a poor start when his stray kick to touch gifted France's Pierre Berbizier a try, Gavin produced a faultless performance, kicking six out of six penalties.

— ROYAL RUGBY PLAYER —

Princess Anne is the patron of the Scottish Rugby Union and an enthusiastic supporter. While a pupil at Gordonstoun School near Elgin, her son Peter Phillips, a quick, nuggety openside flanker, won a cap for Scotland Schools in 1995.

— IT'S RUGBY FIRST FOR RANGERS OWNER —

Sir David Murray may be better known as the owner of Rangers Football Club in Glasgow, but the Old Fettesian's first love was rugby. He was, for many years, on the SRU's advisory board, but resigned when the committee controversially ousted chairman David McKay and chief executive Phil Anderton in January 2005.

— FRENCH CONNECTIONS —

The sport's prime mover in French rugby's early days was Charles Rutherford, a Scottish-born fan of the game who had captained France against Canada in 1902. Despite this, Rutherford, who ran the French Federation, was unable to convince the SFU (the forerunner of the SRU) to play France. Only when the French had played Wales and Ireland first did the SFU change its mind.

— IMPRESSIVE DEBUT —

Gordon Ross holds the record for the biggest number of points scored on a Scotland debut. The fly-half scored 23 points (five penalties and four conversions) in a faultless display of kicking as Scotland beat Tonga 43–20 at Murrayfield in 2002.

— ADOPTED SCOTS —

• The most tenuous qualification to play for Scotland is undoubtedly that of open-side flanker Budge Pountney, who won 31 caps for Scotland between 1998–2002 and even captained his adopted country. Southampton-born Pountney qualified for Scotland through having a grandmother who was born in the Channel Islands, thus giving him the right to plump for whichever of the Home Unions he preferred. His coach at Northampton was former Scotland coach Ian McGeechan – the rest, as they say, is history . . .

• In 1947/48, when the touring Australians beat Scotland by four tries to nil at Murrayfield, the killer third try was set up by Doug Keller. When the young flanker subsequently decided to finish off his medical studies in London, coming from a family of Scots émigrés he decided to join London Scottish. His displays for them were so good that just 14 months later he was not only selected for Scotland but was handed the captaincy in a highly controversial move that eventually led to the IRB tightening up the rules on eligibility.

• The most amusing adoption process came when newly arrived Boroughmuir centre Sean Lineen, son of the famous All Black centre Terry but with no qualifications to play for Scotland, was nonetheless selected to play for the country. Trying to establish his credentials, he was sent up to Stornoway in the Western Isles for a photo opportunity at the site from which his Scottish ancestors apparently hailed. Lineen had taken the time and effort to ask Scotland legend John Jeffrey what he should say to the islanders at the planned reception. Explaining that most of the islanders have gaelic as their first language, they suggested that he use the old local greeting of "pog m'hone". It was only later, after being confronted with a row of shocked faces, that he found out what the 'greeting' meant – "kiss my arse".

— EPIC BARREN SPELL —

Scotland's infamous four-year barren spell lasted from 24th February 1951, when they lost 6–5 at home to Ireland, to 5th February 1955 when a ferocious performance stunned Wales and saw the home side win 14–8. In that time they were beaten 17 times on the hoof, with the 44–0 home loss to the Springboks arguably the worst reversal ever sustained by the national side.

— SCOTLAND'S NZ SUCCESS —

In 1959, Ken Scotland was voted one of New Zealand's five Players of the Year.

— WILLIAMS' WOE —

It is generally held that the least successful Scotland coach was the first non-Scot to be appointed to the job, silver-haired, smooth-talking Aussie Matt Williams.

After taking over after the 2003 World Cup, Williams presided over 17 Scotland matches, of which they won just three – against Samoa, Japan and Italy – before he was fired in April 2005. During that time, Scotland managed just one Six Nations victory and were humiliated at home on several occasions, most notably by Wales.

Williams' tenure was also notable for his notion of a 'Fortress Scotland', a plan where he wanted all of Scotland's top players to be playing north of the border. The former Leinster coach wanted to take Scotland to the 2007 World Cup with every member of the squad playing their rugby in Scotland.

By contrast, Scotland's most effective coaching partnership is generally accepted to have been the combination of Ian McGeechan and Jim Telfer. Having won the 1990 Grand Slam and the final Five Nations Championship in 1999, they also combined to great effect to produce a winning Lions tour to South Africa in 1997.

— CONSECUTIVE TRIES —

In six games between 1906 and 1908, London Scottish wing A.H.B.L. Purves' scored a try in six consecutive games, a Scottish record that has yet to be beaten.

— MACDONALD SEIZES THE MOMENT —

London Scottish centre Gordon Macdonald seized the moment in 1969 to become a one-cap wonder – but he could so easily have ended his career with no caps at all. Selected on the bench to face Ireland during that year's Six Nations match at Murrayfield, the match was almost over when star three-quarter Chris Rea was injured.

However, the selectors were particularly parsimonious when it came to handing out caps and had no intention of allowing the Exile to win his first cap, particularly as Scotland were coasting to a 16–0 victory. With the clock ticking down, Macdonald took matters into his own hands, running to the touchline and catching the referee's attention. Before any of the men in blazers could stop him, the referee waved him on and he charged on to win his first cap. You don't thumb your nose at the Murrayfield high heidyins, though – it also proved to be the one and only time he appeared for Scotland.

— SCOTTISH RULES —

Scottish administrators were very conspicuous in the game's early development. Although the first codified laws were those written down at Rugby School in 1846, the next set of laws were those of Edinburgh Academy in 1858 (which gave rise to the so-called 'Little Green Book'). The English tried to rewrite the laws in 1862 with the Blackheath Rules, but the Scots amended them hugely with the laws of Blairgowrie, Rattray and Neigbourhood in 1865, having yet another say with the 'Kilmarnock FC Rules of Play' in 1869.

— RUGBY'S ARCHITECT —

One of the five men who put his name to the 1870 challenge to the English that led to the first international (see *The First International: The Challenge*, page 2) was Merchistonian FC captain Benjamin Hall Blyth. The architect and engineer later went on to design the clubhouse at Muirfield golf course, and to design Gullane No.1 golf course and the New Course at St Andrews. He also designed and built the Tay Bridge, Edinburgh's Waverly Station, the Grange Cricket Club pavilion, Glasgow station and Edinburgh's North Bridge.

— ALMOND IS NUTS FOR RUGBY —

Glaswegian Hely Hutchison Almond is the single most important figure in the development of rugby in Scotland. The "great apostle of muscular Christianity" had been a student at Glasgow University and Balliol College, Oxford before spending a year at Loretto and then moving to Merchiston for four crucial years between 1858–62.

These were crucial years because they coincided with the arrival of fellow Glaswegian and Merchiston headmaster Thomas Harvey and Moffat man John Rogerson, who succeeded Harvey as headmaster at Merchiston in 1863. All four were together at the Edinburgh school for four years and in that time established the game before Almond left for Loretto and Harvey for the Academy. Merchiston was one of the hotbeds of schools rugby for many years, though, and the period during which Rogerson was headmaster at Merchiston (1863–1898) "was remembered as the days of unbeaten rugby sides".

By the end of the 1860s, rugby was being played in at least eight schools and as well as the Glasgow and Edinburgh FP outfits there were also clubs in Alloa, Ayr, Blairgowrie, Dollar, Kilmarnock and Perth.

— THE FIRST MATCH . . . AND IT'S A LONG ONE —

The first match played in Scotland was started in 1857 but finished in 1858. It was between Edinburgh Academy and Edinburgh University and was played between two sides of 25 over four Saturdays, starting on Boxing Day in 1857 and finally concluding on 16th January the next year.

The match took so long to play because the winner was to be the first team to four goals (a try and a successful conversion), but after the students scored one in the first game, the second and third games remained scoreless. Only by upscaling to sides of 30 each and agreeing not to leave until the game was settled did they reach a conclusion, largely because three of the pupils had played in England and had learned to drop kick. Four drop goals in that fourth game settled the issue in the pupils' favour.

— GOOD SCHOOLING —

The school that has turned out the most Scottish internationals is Edinburgh Academy.

— CROWDED SCENE —

The crowd is often referred to as the 16th man, and when Scotland travelled to Swansea in the 1921 Five Nations, that proved to be the case. In fact, the Welsh crowd were credited with gifting Scotland their first win on Welsh soil for 29 years.

The game was played at St Helen's and such was the demand to see the match the terraces were so crammed that the touchline was lined with spectators. All seemed to be going well until six minutes into the game, when Wales were awarded a penalty and Albert Jenkins stepped up to take it. At this point proceedings descended into chaos, with fans spilling out of the stands and onto the pitch, with several running across the pitch itself and, according to contemporary reports, "committing disgraceful acts on the field of play". The players fled to the dressing rooms for a quarter of an hour until a unit of mounted police had managed to disperse the crowd, but the ruckus seemed to unnerve the home side. Jenkins shanked his kick wide of the right post and the Scots, previously under the cosh, went in at half-time leading by 11 points.

The crowd invaded the pitch again during the break, and although the police managed to restore order, the atmosphere was simmering. Wales were doing well on the pitch though, and had drawn to within one score of the lead with two four-point dropped goals from Jenkins. But as Wales laid siege to the Scottish line, there were further incursions from spectators onto the field of play, forcing the referee to call a halt to proceedings. Although the delay was only temporary, Wales never recovered their forward momentum and Scotland ran out winners by 11–8.

— NAME CHANGE —

The Scottish Rugby Union wasn't so called until 1924, the year before the opening of Murrayfield. From its formation until that date it was called the Scottish Football Union.

— SCHOOLBOY FOES —

In 1880, Edinburgh Academy schoolboys Charles Reid and Frank Wright, both still 17, found themselves on opposing sides in the second Calcutta Cup game – Reid for Scotland and Wright, a boarder from Manchester, for England.

— SCOTLAND'S GREATEST GAMES 8 —

Scotland 18 Wales 19
Murrayfield
6th February 1971

This was a Scottish campaign dominated by two touchline conversions, one by a Scot, the other against them. The successful conversion which gave the men in blue victory came in injury-time at Twickenham when P.C. Brown, himself a try-scorer earlier in the match, converted Chris Rea's late try to give Scotland a one-point Calcutta Cup victory (they also beat England 26–6 the next week at Murrayfield in the Centenary International, giving them a unique double).

The other kick was an even more famous *coup de grâce*, one which not only assumed an importance of biblical proportions in Wales, but which capped one of the best Five Nations matches of all time: the kick dubbed "the greatest conversion since St Paul".

The match was a classic which kept the crowd of 80,000 in uproar, with Scotland leading four times to Wales' three and neither side managing to establish a lead of more than five points at any stage. It was a clash of styles, with a slick Wales outfit led by possibly the best halfback combination rugby has ever seen in Gareth Edwards and Barry John, both of whom scored sensational solo tries to go with flanker John Taylor's opener, facing a Scottish XV which refused to yield and which was sustained by two determined, bullocking runs from Chris Rea and Sandy Carmichael which both resulted in tries.

For much of the match the game had been a kicking duel between P.C. Brown for Scotland and John and Taylor for Wales (right-footed John from the left, left-footed Taylor from the right). But when Rea crashed over for the second Scottish try, even though P.C. missed the conversion it left the home side four points ahead with just seconds left on the clock.

And that's when the drama became almost unbearable. Launching a series of last-gasp attacks, Wales won a line-out on the left touchline just short of Scotland's 25 and Delme Thomas palmed to Edwards, the ball passing to Barry John, who threw a miss-pass to full back J.P.R. Williams, who had steamed into the line. He fed quicksilver wing Gerald Davies who was able to tiptoe down the right touchline and, under huge pressure from would-be tacklers, dot the ball down in the corner. It was a breathless climax to a marvellous match but there was more to come as Taylor lined up the biggest kick of his life before knocking over a conversion that was enough to keep Wales on track for their first Grand Slam since 1952.

— SCOTLAND LEGENDS XV: CHARLES REID —

Charles 'Hippo' Reid made his debut against Ireland while still a schoolboy and aged just 17 years and 36 days, although the great Ninian Finlay, who made his debut at exactly the same age (to the day) appears in the records as the youngest player to pull on a Scotland shirt by dint of having lived through one less leap year than Reid.

A giant of a man, at 6ft 3in and 16 stones, Reid dwarfed virtually all of his contemporaries. Yet it is not for his sheer size that he was known but for his skill, courage and determination. He had good hands, was a tough tackler and one of the foremost exponents of the art of dribbling. His peers reckoned him the best forward of his generation and his stats certainly bear that out: Scotland only lost four times in his 21 caps and in 1887 he skippered his country to their first Championship. He even managed to get on the scoresheet with four tries.

Rugby was in Reid's genes. Even before he made his debut his older brother James had won five caps for Scotland, playing alongside the great 'Bulldog' Irvine, a player who retired from the game before Hippo's debut. Yet the team in which Reid played was stuffed with some of the greatest players ever to play for Scotland, men like Lions skipper Bill Maclagan and peerless centre Ninian Finlay, not to mention legendary low-slung halfback Andrew Don Wauchope.

On the opposite side to Reid on his debut was his close friend and classmate Frank Wright, a boarder from Manchester, who was a late call-up for England in 1881 in the drawn match at Raeburn Place. The two boys were carried shoulder-high by a cheering mob when they returned to the Academy. It was at school that Reid earned his nickname of 'Hippo' – not for his size but because he didn't know the word for 'horse' when asked in a Greek lesson.

Charles Reid vital statistics
Caps: 21 (1881–88)
Position: Second row
Club: Edinburgh Academicals

— SATURDAY FIRST —

The first international match to be played on a Saturday was Scotland versus Ireland at Hamilton Crescent in 1880. Until then, all international matches were played on Mondays.

— SCOTS ON FIRST TOUR —

Two Scots took part in the first ever major rugby tour, which was staged by professional cricketers Alfred Shaw and Arthur Shrewsbury and went to Australia and New Zealand in 1888. On the tour, they not only played rugby, but also the Victorian code – the early Australian Rules Football. Brothers W. Burnet and R. Burnet were both Hawick men, as was A.J. Laing. Two Edinburgh University students also accompanied the tour.

— 1,000TH CAP —

Leicester lock Jim Hamilton was the 1,000th man to be capped for Scotland when he made his debut against England in 2007. Between 1871 and 1993, only 845 players had been capped (an average of less than seven new caps each year). Since 1993, the liberal use of replacements and the expanded programme of international rugby has seen over 150 players make their Scotland debuts at a rate of over 11 new caps each season.

— OLD STAGERS —

The oldest man to make his Scotland debut was Northampton full back Tom Gray, who first represented his country in the 13–11 Calcutta Cup victory at Murrayfield in 1950 when aged 33 years and two months. He scored two conversions. Another notable oldie was Dunfermline's Ron Glasgow, who didn't win a cap until he was 31 but went on to win another nine, playing until he was 34.

He isn't the oldest man to play for Scotland, though. That privilege went to legendary Jordanhill and British Lions prop Ian 'Mighty Mouse' McLauchlan, who was 37 years and six months by the time he hung up his boots after winning his 43rd and final cap more than ten years after making his debut in the 1967 8–3 loss to England at Twickenham. McLauchlan's career bears an uncanny resemblance to that of another Scottish veteran, second row Ally McHarg, a man who also hung his boots up in 1979 after also making 43 appearances for his country. The West of Scotland and London Scottish hardman packed down on 35 occasions behind McLauchlan, with neither of the two players missing a game for the six-year period from 1971–76. For seven of those years, the two of them played alongside West of Scotland and British Lions lock Gordon Brown, who played with either McHarg or McLauchlan in every one of his 30 Scotland caps.

— McHARG'S FOOLHARDY MOMENT —

Scotland lock Ally McHarg remains either the bravest or most foolhardy man ever to have pulled on a Scotland shirt.

As a fresh-faced youngster with a reputation for getting his retaliation in first, he found himself facing veteran All Black hardman Colin 'Pinetrees' Meads, a legend of the 1950s and 1960s. There was, he thought, only one thing to do: so at the first line-out, McHarg leaned over and lamped Meads as hard as he could.

As soon as the punch connected with the Kiwi's jaw, there was a stunned pause in play as Meads shook his head. Otherwise uninjured and certainly unruffled, Meads contemplated his worried-looking opponent and slowly and deliberately uttered the immortal lines: "McHarg! I'm gonna kill you!" Only 75 minutes of evasive action from the young Scot saved his skin . . .

— THE FIRST ANGLO-SCOT —

At the time of the first international in 1871, Merchistonian A.G. Colville had been playing in London for Blackheath for three years and was considered one of the finest players in the game. He was invited to play for England, but turned down the option, appearing for Scotland instead. He turned out to be playing against a countryman and fellow Blackheath player, B.H. Burns, a Perthshire-born banker who went to school at Edinburgh Academy and university in St Andrews, but who accepted an invitation to turn out for England.

— WINGER SINGER —

Scotland Sevens speedster Thom Evans took a year out of rugby between playing for Wasps and Glasgow to join a boyband, Twen2y4Se7en, touring as a support act with McFly, Peter Andre and Westlife throughout 2004.

A scratch golfer who also sprinted for England Schools before adopting the land of his grandfather's birth, the wing comes from a sporting family: his mother Sally was South Africa's top 100m sprinter and his father Brian was a professional golfer who won several tournaments on the European Tour. Brother Max is also a professional rugby player, having also joined Glasgow Warriors.

— CRICKETING CROSS-OVER —

Cricket and rugby have long been intertwined in Scotland, with many famous club grounds in Glasgow and Edinburgh such as Raeburn Place, Hamilton Crescent, Inverleith, Myreside and Anniesland being used for both sports.

There has also been a similar cross-over among many players. Recent internationals Hugo Southwell, Duncan Hodge and Gordon Ross, for example, have all played first-class cricket, Southwell in the County Championship for Sussex. All told, 34 Scotland rugby internationals have also played for their country at cricket. Some notable dual-internationals include Scotland and Lions captain Bill Maclagan, pre-war Scotland skippers Andrew Don-Wauchope and scrum-half Ross Logan, father and son J.H. and Rab Bruce-Lockhart, *The Scotsman's* inestimable former rugby correspondent Norman Mair, and arguably the best full back ever to play for the boys in blue, Ken Scotland. Winger Norman Davidson also deserves a special mention for his famous feat of smacking five boundaries in one over to win a club game.

The full list of dual internationals is as follows:

A. Buchanan (Royal High School FP, 1871)
T.R. Marshall (Edinburgh Academicals, 1871–74)
T. Chalmers (Glasgow Academicals, 1871–76)
L.M. Balfour (Edinburgh Academicals, 1872)
E.M. Bannerman (Edinburgh Academicals, 1872–73)
W. St. C. Grant (Craigmount, 1873–74)
J.S. Carrick (Glasgow Academicals, 1876–77)
D. Somerville (Edinburgh Institute FP, 1879–84)
W.E. Maclagan (Edinburgh Academicals, 1878–90)
A.R. Don-Wauchope (Fettesian-Lorretonians, 1881–88)
T. Anderson (Merchiston, 1882)
F. Hunter (Edinburgh University, 1882)
J.G. Walker (West of Scotland, 1882–83)
A.G.G. Asher (Oxford University, 1882–86)
H.J. Stevenson (Edinburgh Academicals, 1888–93)
G. MacGregor (Cambridge University, 1890–96)
A.W. Duncan (Edinburgh University 1901–02)
M.R. Dickson (Edinburgh University 1905)
J.M. Tennent (West of Scotland, 1909–10)
A.W. Angus (Watsonians, 1909–20)
J.H. Bruce-Lockhart (London Scottish, 1913–20)
G.B. Crole (Oxford University, 1920)

T.M. Hart (Glasgow University, 1930)

W.R. Logan (Edinburgh University and Edinburgh Wanderers, 1931–37)

A.S.B. McNeil (Watsonians, 1935)

K.W. Marshall (Edinburgh Academicals, 1934–37)

J.M. Kerr (Heriot's FP, 1935–37)

R.B. Bruce-Lockhart (Cambridge University and London Scottish, 1937–39)

I.J.M. Lumsden (Bath, Watsonians, 1947–49)

N.G.R. Mair (Edinburgh University, 1951)

J.N.G. Davidson (Edinburgh University, 1952–54)

K.J.F. Scotland (Heriot's FP, Cambridge University and Leicester, 1957–65)

D.L. Bell (Watsonians, 1975)

A.B.M. Ker (Kelso, 1988)

— SYMPATHETIC BOSS —

Ah, the good old amateur days! When Scotland and Glasgow High School FP's Grand Slam-winning hooker Jimmy Ireland went to his boss at the Singer Factory to request a Saturday off to make his home debut in the Calcutta Cup match against England at Murrayfield in March 1925 – a match in which a win would give the unbeaten Scots a clean sweep in the tournament – his boss's reply was "Do you really need to take a whole day?"

— BACK IN ACTION AFTER THE WAR —

Only two players managed to appear for Scotland either side of the Second World War. W.B. Young was the only member of the 1938 Triple Crown side to be capped after the war, against England in 1948, while W.C.W. Murdoch (Hillhead High School FP), having won five caps at full back between 1935–39, was recalled for the 1948/49 season. Strangely, despite losing 30 players in the First World War (see *The Ultimate Sacrifice*, page 26), the decade immediately after the conflict was one of Scotland's best rugby periods, the record reading: played 41, won 25, lost 14, drawn 2.

— BIG LADS —

Used to being undersized and underpowered, particularly when compared with the forwards put out by teams such as England, South Africa and France, Scotland found themselves in an unusual situation in the 2007 Six Nations when their pack outweighed England by two stones in the Calcutta Cup clash at Twickenham. They were also taller than any previous Scotland side.

Leading the charge was 6ft 8in Scotland debutant James Hamilton, who weighed in at over 20 stones and played alongside 6ft 8in Ally Kellock, who tipped the scales at 18 stones. Not far behind him was Scotland tighthead prop Euan Murray, another man-mountain at 18 stones 12lbs and 6ft 1in. Indeed, in every game during the 2007 Six Nations, Scotland put out a heavier and/or taller side than ever before, with the heaviest, and often the tallest, players in several positions: second row (Hamilton at over 20 stones), prop (Murray at almost 19 stones), flanker (Simon Taylor at 6ft 5in and nearly 18 stones), centre (Rob Dewey at 6ft 3in and 17stones) and on both wings (Nikki Walker at 6ft 4in and 16 stone 12lbs on one wing, Sean Lamont at 6ft 2in and 16 stone 8lbs on the other).

Those sort of monster stats are in stark contrast to the numbers of earlier generations. When Scotland second row Mike Campbell-Lamerton captained the British Lions on their tour to New Zealand in 1966, he was famously the biggest and heaviest lock Scotland had ever had. He stood 6ft 5in, with his weight coming in at around 17 stones. Yet Campbell-Lamerton's predecessor in the Scotland boiler house had been lock Hamish Kemp who won 27 caps between 1954 and 1960 despite only being 6ft if he stood on tip-toes and weighing in at just under 14 stone – hardly big by the standards of Scotland's backs in 2007, let alone the forwards.

— LOST FOR WORDS —

Two Scots have commented on members of their family scoring important tries for their country. Commentary box legend Bill McLaren was famously overcome when his son-in-law, scrum-half Alan Lawson, scored two tries against England in 1976. In 2007, former Scotland and Lions No.8 John Beattie was the man with the mic as his son Johnnie Beattie, also a No.8, crashed over for a try against Romania on his debut.

— SCOTLAND'S GREATEST GAMES 9 —

France 22 Scotland 36
Stade de France, Paris
10th April 1999

Even though France had performed fitfully in 1999 while Scotland had already beaten Wales and Ireland and should have beaten England at Twickenham, this was a result as utterly unexpected as Scotland's panning of England at Twickenham 13 years earlier, and every bit as stunning. In 1986 Scotland sparred with the English, registering nine points before the break and then going to score 24 in the second half; this time the split was even more dramatic, with Scotland scoring 33 points in the first half and just three in the second. France failed to score in the second half after the highest-scoring half in Five Nations history ended 33–22.

Scotland didn't know it when they took the field that Saturday for their first visit to the Stade de France, but it was a win that was to see them finish top of the final Five Nations Championship when England were beaten in the dying seconds of their match with Wales the next day. Perhaps that is as well because, shorn of any expectations of silverware after the 24–21 defeat in the Calcutta Cup, the Scots played with a verve and fluency that was as startling as it was surprising.

The match didn't start auspiciously for Scotland when their nemesis Emile Ntamack, the wing whose last second try at the 1995 World Cup effectively put the Scots out of the competition, scored after just two minutes. But rather than go into their shells, the hugely experienced collection of Scotland caps went on to the offensive and ran at their hosts with an energy and directness that has rarely been seen from Scotland teams.

First Martin Leslie touched down for his first try after a break from Kenny Logan. Then Alan Tait went over after a coruscating break from man of the match Glenn Metcalfe. Finally, Brive No.10 Gregor Townsend broke through for a splendid solo try that was his fourth of the Championship – he'd scored in each match – and which the French spectators greeted with whistles and catcalls.

Not that Scotland had finished. France flanker Christophe Juillet notched a reply for the home side but then Metcalfe broke the thin blue line once again to put Tait in before Martin Leslie rounded off a surreal 35 minutes with his second try and Scotland's fifth, Logan's conversion making it 33–12.

Although France hit back with a try by Christophe Dominici and a penalty from Daniel Aucagne, their heart wasn't in the chase and a low-key second half was played out with no movement on the scoreboard save for one Logan penalty.

When Scotland beat France in Paris in 1995 courtesy of the Toony flip to end 26 years of losses in Paris, they left it late. Four years later, they hit hard and early for one of the most amazing results in Scottish rugby history.

— LONGEST TIME BETWEEN CAPS —

Alan Tait holds the record for the longest period between caps at eight years, 361 days between 1988 and 1997.

W.C.W. 'Copey' Murdoch won five caps between 1935–39 and then had to wait eight years, 312 days to collect his next cap. A versatile player, he won a total of nine caps, appearing at centre, wing and full back over a record 14 seasons.

— FRENCH REVENGE —

France got revenge for their last-gasp Five Nations home defeat by Scotland in 1995 when the two sides met in Pretoria's Loftus Versfeld Stadium at the World Cup later that year. The two sides had already played out one epic 20–20 draw in their only previous World Cup meeting, and there was a recent history of nail-bitingly close matches between the two sides. Scotland were leading 19–15, with just seconds left when French wing Emile Ntamack snaked across the pitch, making for the corner, and rode through Rob Wainwright's tackle to dot down in the corner and sneak the win.

— LOOSE CHANGE —

In the 1991 World Cup, Scotland's players were paid £368.80 each to compete in the tournament.

— SCOTTISH OWNERS DOWN SOUTH —

There are two Scots who own English Guinness Premiership clubs: Double glazing tycoon Brian Kennedy at Sale Sharks and motorsport entrepreneur Tom Walkinshaw at Gloucester.

— KILLED IN ACTION —

The following Scotland internationals lost their lives fighting for their country:

Boer War (1899–1902):
1900: D.B. Monypenny (London Scottish, 1888–9)

First World War (1914–18):
1914: R.F. Simson (London Scottish, 1911); J.L. Huggan (London Scottish, 1914); J. Ross (London Scottish, 1901–3); L. Robertson (London Scottish, 1908–13)
1915: F.H. Turner (Oxford University, Liverpool, 1911–14); J. Pearson (Watsonians, 1909–13); D. McL. Bain (Oxford University, 1911–14); W.C. Church (Glasgow Academicals, 1906); E.T. Young (Glasgow Academicals, 1914); P.C.B. Blair (Cambridge University, 1912–13); W.M. Wallace (Cambridge University, 1913–14); D.R. Bedell-Sivright (Cambridge University, Edinburgh University, 1900–1908); W.M. Dickson (Blackheath, Oxford University, 1912–13)
1916: D.D. Howie (Kirkcaldy, 1912–13); A. Ross (Royal HSFP, 1905-9); C.H. Abercrombie (United Services, 1910–13); J.S. Wilson (United Services, London Scottish, 1908–09); R. Fraser (Cambridge University, 1911); E. Milroy (Watsonians, 1910–14)
1917: J.G. Will (Cambridge University, 1912–14); T.A .Nelson (Oxford University, 1898); W.T. Forrest (Hawick, 1903–5); A.L. Wade (London Scottish, 1908); J.Y.M. Henderson (Watsonians, 1911); J.A. Campbell (West of Scotland, 1878–81); S.S.L. Steyn (Oxford University, 1911–12)
1918: G.A.W. Lamond (Kelvinside Academicals, 1899–1905); W.R. Hutchison (Glasgow HSFP, 1911); R.E. Gordon (Royal Artillery, 1913); W.R. Sutherland (Hawick, 1910–14)

Second World War (1939–45):
1940: D.K.A. MacKenzie (Edinburgh Wanderers, 1939)
1941: T.F. Dorward (Gala, 1938–9); A.W. Symington (Cambridge University, 1914)
1942: P. Munro (Oxford University, London Scottish, 1905–11); J.M. Ritchie (Watsonians, 1933–34); R.M. Kinnear (Heriot's FP, 1926); W.A. Ross (Hillhead HSFP, 1937); J.G.S. Forrest (Cambridge University, 1938); S. St. C. Ford (United Services, Royal Navy, 1930–32)
1943: G. Roberts (Watsonians, 1938–39); W.M. Penman (RAF, 1939)
1944: A.S.B. McNeil (Watsonians, 1935); W.N. Renwick (London Scottish, Edinburgh Wanderers, 1938–39); G.H. Gaille (Edinburgh Academicals, 1939)
1945: E.H. Liddell (Edinburgh University, 1922–23)

— SCOTLAND LEGENDS XV: GARY ARMSTRONG —

Gary Armstrong: the archetypal Borders terrier

When they were team-mates Jonny Wilkinson's nickname for Gary Armstrong "was Scrap Yard Dog . . . because I've never met anyone as tough as him", while the scrum-half is widely known as Jim Telfer's favourite player, which pretty much says it all.

Tough and committed, he was the archetypal Borders terrier, snapping at the heels of opposition players when they had the ball, searching for holes in the opposition's defences when he had it. Neither showy nor overly voluble, Armstrong's game was by no means flawless, with a pass that was laboured and of varying accuracy, but his strengths and unquenchable spirit more than made up for any technical deficiencies.

Those qualities were seen on numerous occasions, most notably during the 1990 Grand Slam game in tandem with regular half-back partner Craig Chalmers, but were in evidence throughout his career, including the period in 1997–98 when the former lorry driver was recruited by Newcastle and immediately helped them to the English League title.

Armstrong was beloved of coaches for being the sort of player who would put his head down and just get on with it. On the Lions tour to Australia in 1989, Welshman Robert Jones was preferred to Armstrong but the Borderer worked as hard as ever and never complained. Similarly, when a succession of injuries threatened his career in 1992 and 1995, he didn't bleat but just got on with his rehabilitation, coming back strongly enough to fight off the twin challenges of Andy Nicol and Bryan Redpath.

Armstrong's career ended on a high note in 1999 when, in his last Five Nations, he captained Scotland to a remarkable Championship-topping season that could have been another Grand Slam if Scotland had played the first 20 minutes at Twickenham in the same way that they had played the last 60. By the time Armstrong retired he was 37 and the wheel had gone full circle: at the start of his career, he had supplanted JedForest legend Roy Laidlaw; at the end of his career and while with the Borders, he in turn was overtaken by future British Lions No.9 Chris Cusiter. In true Armstrong style he did all he could to mentor the young scrum-half.

Gary Armstrong vital statistics
Caps: 51 (1988–99)
Position: Scrum-half
Clubs: JedForest, Newcastle Falcons, Borders

— PAINFUL CONVERSION —

Eric Liddell isn't the only born-again Christian to have played for Scotland. Tighthead prop Euan Murray also found God after a nasty blow to the head playing against Munster.

"A year ago I accepted Jesus into my life, and it's changed everything for me," he said in February 2007. "I got a really bad knock against Munster and it just made me wake up and take a look at myself. I didn't like what I saw. Now I feel more positive, more secure, more settled; my faith has given me a sense of peace and inner calm that's completely changed the way I approach life. Not that being a Christian makes you a weak person, that'd never work in this game."

— LOST IN TRANSLATION —

In 1995, Scotland went into the final seconds of their match at the Parc de Princes without a win in Paris since 1969 and trailing by 21–16. That was when Gregor Townsend, who led the final attack of the game, took out two French would-be tacklers with a reverse pop pass, which immediately became known as the 'Toony Flip', leaving Gavin Hastings free to run 40 yards and dot the ball down under the posts.

That night, as is customary, Scotland skipper Gavin Hastings was due to make a speech at the after-match dinner. He had decided that it might win a few hearts and minds if he made the speech in French, although there was one small problem – he knew virtually nothing of the language. In desperation he turned to Damian 'Del Boy' Cronin, who had been playing in France with Bourges.

Cronin agreed to translate, and Hastings soon found himself rising up from the top table to make a speech with the big second row relaying his words to his hosts in their mother tongue. That's when it all went wrong. "Ladies and gentlemen, it gives me great pleasure to stand here before you," he said. "I thank you for your kind hospitality after a mad, passionate game," which was the point at which virtually the whole room burst into laughter and all the French speakers rose as one man to give him a standing ovation. Cronin had translated his opening as follows: "Ladies and gentlemen, it gives me great pleasure to tell you that as soon as I finish this speech I am looking forward to taking my wife upstairs and having mad, passionate sex with her."

— FIRST TRY SCORER —

The first try in international rugby was a pushover try by Royal HSFP's Angus Buchanan for Scotland against England at Raeburn Place on 27th March 1871. Buchanan later went on to play cricket for Scotland.

— SELECTION GAMBLE PAYS OFF —

The biggest gamble by a group of selectors? Surely it has to be in 1901 when Scotland selected eight students – seven of them uncapped and one with one cap – for their opening international against Wales. The seven uncapped students were all from Edinburgh University, with five of them being backs. The result? An entirely unexpected 18–8 win against a Wales side that had arrived with high expectations.

— TOWNSEND'S TOP XV —

Asked to nominate the best players he ever played with or against, Gregor Townsend made one surprising choice in little known Ivory Coast flanker Ishmail Lassisi, a player who France wanted to select but who had already won one cap for his homeland.

Townsend's full team contained five New Zealanders and lines up as follows:

```
15 Christian Cullen (New Zealand)
14 Rupeni Caucaubaci (Fiji)
13 Brian O'Driscoll (Ireland)
12 Tim Horan (Australia)
11 Jonah Lomu (New Zealand)
10 Gregor Townsend (Scotland)
 9 Rob Howley (Wales)
 1 Tom Smith (Scotland)
 2 Keith Wood (Ireland
 3 Craig Dowd (New Zealand)
 4 Martin Johnson (England)
 5 John Eales (Australia)
 6 Ishmail Lassisi (Ivory Coast)
 7 Richie McCaw (New Zealand)
 8 Zinzan Brooke (New Zealand)
```

Coaches: Jim Telfer and Ian McGeechan.

— SCOTTISH BY NAME —

Several Scotland internationals have names that come from towns or geographical features north of the border: Bill Scott, Pat Munro, Mike Biggar, Jim Hamilton, Ron Glasgow, Ken Scotland, W.F. Blackadder, J.B. Borthwick, Finlay and Jim Calder, Gary Callandar, G.N. Cathcart, J.A. Crawford, L.R. Currie, Rob Cunningham, Jon Dunbar, Doug Elliot, Quentin Dunlop, W.S. Glen, Andy Irvine, William Lauder, David Leslie, Iain Paxton, Adam Roxburgh, AV Symington, Jock Wemyss.

Although not named after Scottish towns, Jimmy Ireland, Gavin and Scott Hastings, John Dallas and Willie Welsh all deserve a mention in dispatches.

— TEAM OF MANY CLUBS —

The 1984 Grand Slam-winning side that took the field in the game against France contained players from ten different clubs. The only clubs that had more than one representative were Hawick (3), Selkirk (2) and Gala (3). The team was as follows: Peter Dods (Gala); Jim Pollock (Gosforth), Keith Robertson (Melrose), David Johnston (Watsonians), Roger Baird (Kelso); John Rutherford (Selkirk), Roy Laidlaw (Jedforest); Jim Aitken (Gala, captain), Colin Deans (Hawick), Iain Milne (Heriot's FP), A.J. Campbell (Hawick), Alan Tomes (Hawick), David Leslie (Gala), Jim Calder (Stewart's-Melville FP), Iain Paxton (Selkirk).

The 1990 Grand Slam starting team had players from 13 different clubs. The only players who played their club rugby together were the three London Scots. The team was as follows: Gavin Hastings (London Scottish); Tony Stanger (Hawick); Sean Lineen (Boroughmuir), Scott Hastings (Watsonians), Iwan Tukalo (Selkirk); Craig Chalmers (Melrose), Gary Armstrong (Jedforest); David Sole (Edinburgh Academicals, captain), Kenny Milne (Heriot's FP), Paul Burnell (London Scottish), Damian Cronin (Bath), Chris Gray (Nottingham), John Jeffrey (Kelso), Finlay Calder (Stewart's-Melville FP), Derek White (London Scottish)

— ALL CHANGE —

Scotland's change strip is traditionally white. The only time this varied was during the period when Cotton Oxford were the shirt manufacturers in 1998–1999. The new change strip was first unveiled when Scotland took the field against the New Zealand Maori in November 1998 wearing an orange shirt with blue hoops on the sleeves. Cotton Oxford also introduced purple flashes onto the main strip, a practice which didn't last beyond the end of their two-year contract with the SRU.

— WHISTLE-BLOWER —

London Scottish full back Pat Harrower won one cap against Wales in 1885, but he has a far more interesting claim to fame. He also refereed the 1905 FA Cup final between Aston Villa and Newcastle United at Crystal Palace. For the record, the Brummies won 2–0, with Harry Hampton scoring both goals.

— SCOTLAND AT THE WORLD CUP: 2003, AUSTRALIA —

2003 was the low point of Scotland's World Cup campaigns. It started badly with an exceptionally laboured win over Japan and continued in similar vein. The win over the US Eagles was also poor and a five-try humping at the hands of France left Scotland needing to beat Fiji in the final game to progress to the knockout stages. In the end, it was a horribly close-run thing, with full back Glenn Metcalfe having to put in two try-saving tackles on wing Rupeni Caucaubaci to keep Scotland in the game. Even then, with seconds left on the clock, Caucau's two tries to Chris Paterson's five penalties meant that Scotland were still behind and just about to go out at the pool stages for the first time when, with Fiji reduced to 14 men, prop Tom Smith was driven over from close range in a frantic finale that saw Scotland draw level, with Paterson's conversion giving them the win.

Scotland were just never in the quarter-final against hosts Australia, and although the first half finished tryless, Australia scored tries through Mortlock, Gregan and Lyons in the third quarter before hooker Robbie Russell scored a consolation try in injury-time. It had been an unhappy, injury-ridden tour in which coach Ian McGeechan accused the Wallaby management of spying on their training sessions ("I can honestly tell you I don't even know where they're training," replied Australia coach Eddie Jones) and which was characterised by dire relations with the press. The tour party also had the embarrassment of having to move hotels twice, the first time to avoid a gang of Hell's Angels bikers called the Bandidos who were sharing their Gold Coast hotel, the second time to avoid a wedding party.

Pool matches:
Scotland 32 Japan 11
Scotland 39 United States 15
Scotland 9 France 51
Scotland 22 Fiji 20

Quarter-final:
Scotland 16 Australia 33

— NON-SCORING WINGER —

In 27 tests between 1981–88, Kelso wing Roger Baird never managed to score a try for Scotland – but he did get on the scoresheet for the British Lions.

— HEADLESS, WAGGA AND TOO TALL —

Rugby players have often given each other obscure nicknames, and the custom hasn't changed. Here is a selection of current monikers:

Nathan Hines (Wagga)
Chris Paterson (Mossy)
Martin Leslie (Headless)
Richard Metcalfe (Too Tall)
Gordon Ross (Goggsy)
Allan Jacobsen (Chunk)

Nicknames of past stars include:

Charles Reid (Hippo)
David Bedell-Sivright (Darkie)
Matthew McEwan (Saxon)
Robert Irvine (Bulldog)
Jim Telfer (Creamy)
Ian McGeechan (Geech)
Ian McLauchlan (Mighty Mouse)
Ian Milne (The Bear)
Peter Wright (Teapot)
Bryan Redpath (Basil)
Gregor Townsend (Toony)
Damian Cronin (Del Boy)
Paul Burnell (Archie)

— THAT'S MA DONNA —

The most capped player in Scotland is a woman. Royal High Corstorphine No.8 Donna Kennedy, the captain of Scotland's women, won her 100th cap against France in the final game of the 2007 Six Nations.

— UNCAPPED LIONS —

Three players have been uncapped by Scotland when chosen to tour with the British Lions: J.C. Hosack (Edinburgh Wanderers, toured in 1903 to South Africa), Dr W.A. Robertson (Edinburgh University and Hartlepool Rovers, toured in 1910 to South Africa), and C.G. Timms (Edinburgh University, toured in 1910 to South Africa).

— SCOTTISH LIONS —

Well in excess of 100 Scots have toured with the British Isles Touring XV, better known as the British Lions. They are as follows:

1888 to Australia and New Zealand:
W. Burnet (Hawick), R. Burnet (Hawick), A.J. Laing (Hawick), Dr H. Brooks (Edinburgh University, Durham), Dr J. Smith (Edinburgh University)

The Burnets were brothers and along with club-mate A.J. Laing had their expenses closely examined by the Scottish Football Union, as the SRU was known until 1925. This was to ensure that they upheld the strict principles of amateurism. Although no action was taken it appears as if the committee members were not entirely convinced. There is no evidence that Brooks or Smith were Scots, and none of these five players were capped by Scotland.

1891 to South Africa
Bill Maclagan (London Scottish, captain), Paul Clauss (Oxford University), Robert 'Judy' Macmillan (London Scottish), Willie Wotherspoon (Cambridge University)

1896 to South Africa
No Scots selected

1899 to Australia
Alfred Boucher (Edinburgh Accies), Alec Timms (Edinburgh University)

This was the first tour to include capped players from all four Unions.

1903 to South Africa
Mark Morrison (Royal HSFP, captain), David Bedell-Sivright (Cambridge University), Jimmy Gillespie (Edinburgh Accies), Louis Greig (United Services), JC Hosack (Edinburgh Wanderers), Robert Neill (Edinburgh Accies), Bill Scott (West of Scotland)

1904 to Australia and New Zealand
David Bedell-Sivright (Cambridge University, captain).

1908 to Australia and New Zealand
Entirely Anglo-Welsh selection.

1910 to South Africa
Eric Milroy (Watsonians), James Reid-Kerr (Greenock Wanderers), Dr W.A. Robertson (Edinburgh University and Hartlepool Rovers) Louis Speirs (Watsonians) R.C. Stevenson (St Andrews University), C.G. Timms (Edinburgh University)

1924 to South Africa
Doug Davies (Hawick), Dan Drysdale (George Heriot's FP), Robert Henderson (Northern), Kelvin Hendrie (George Heriot's FP), Bob Howie (Kirkcaldy), Roy Kinnear (George Heriot's FP), Neil Macpherson (Newport), Andrew Ross (Kilmarnock), Ian Smith (Oxford University), Herbert Waddell (Glasgow Accies)

1930 to Australia and New Zealand
Willie Welsh (Hawick)

1938 to South Africa
Laurie Duff (Glasgow Accies), Duncan Macrae (St Andrews University), Jock Waters (Selkirk)

1950 to Australia and New Zealand
Gus Black (Edinburgh University), Peter Kininmonth (Oxford University and Richmond), Ranald Macdonald (Edinburgh University), Doug Smith (London Scottish)

1955 to South Africa
Angus Cameron (Glasgow HSFP), Tom Elliot (Gala), Jim Greenwood (Dunfermline), Hughie McLeod (Hawick), Ernie Michie (Aberdeen University), Arthur Smith (Cambridge University)

1959 to Australia and New Zealand
Stan Coughtrie (Edinburgh Accies), Hughie McLeod (Hawick), Ken Scotland (George Heriot's FP), Ken Smith (Kelso), Gordon Waddell (Cambridge University)

1962 to South Africa
Arthur Smith (Edinburgh Wanderers, captain), Mike Campbell-Lamerton (Army, Halifax), Ronnie Cowan (Selkirk), John Douglas (Daniel Stewart's College FP), Dave Rollo (Howe of Fife), Gordon Waddell (London Scottish)

1966 to Australia and New Zealand
Mike Campbell-Lamerton (London Scottish, captain), Derrick Grant (Hawick), Frank Laidlaw (Melrose), Sandy Hinshelwood (London Scottish), Jim Telfer (Melrose), Stewart Wilson (London Scottish)

1968 to South Africa
Rodger Arneil (Edinburgh Accies), Gordon Connell (London Scottish), Sandy Hinshelwood (London Scottish), Peter Stagg (Sale), Jim Telfer (Melrose), Jock Turner (Gala)

1971 to Australia and New Zealand
Rodger Arneil (Leicester), Alastair Biggar (London Scottish), Gordon Brown (West of Scotland), Sandy Carmichael (West of Scotland), Frank Laidlaw (Melrose), Ian McLauchlan (Jordanhill), Chris Rea (Headingly)

1974 to South Africa
Gordon Brown (West of Scotland), Sandy Carmichael (West of Scotland), Andy Irvine (George Heriot's FP), Ian McGeechan (Headingly), Ian McLauchlan (Jordanhill), Billy Steele (Bedford and RAF)

1977 to New Zealand and Fiji
Gordon Brown (West of Scotland), Bruce Hay (Boroughmuir), Andy Irvine (George Heriot's FP), Ian McGeechan (Headingly), Dougie Morgan (Stewart's/Melville FP)

1980 to South Africa
John Beattie (Glasgow Accies), Bruce Hay (Boroughmuir), Andy Irvine (George Heriot's FP), Jim Renwick (Hawick), Alan Tomes (Hawick)

1983 to New Zealand
Roger Baird (Kelso); John Beattie (Glasgow Accies), Jim Calder (Stewart's/Melville FP), Colin Deans (Hawick), Roy Laidlaw (Jedforest), Iain Milne (George Heriot's FP), Iain Paxton (Selkirk), John Rutherford (Selkirk)

1989 to Australia
Finlay Calder (Stewart's/Melville FP, captain), Gary Armstrong (Jedforest), Craig Chalmers (Melrose), Peter Dods (Gala), Gavin Hastings (Watsonians), Scott Hastings (Watsonians), John Jeffrey (Kelso), David Sole (Edinburgh Accies), Derek White (London Scottish)

1993 to New Zealand
Gavin Hastings (Watsonians, captain), Paul Burnell (London Scottish), Damian Cronin (London Scottish), Scott Hastings (Watsonians), Kenny Milne (George Heriot's FP), Andy Nicol (Dundee HSFP), Andy Reed (Bath), Peter Wright (Boroughmuir).

1997 to South Africa
Tom Smith (Caldeonia Reds), Tony Stanger (Hawick), Alan Tait (Newcastle), Gregor Townsend (Northampton), Rob Wainwright (Caledonia Reds), Doddie Weir (Newcastle)

2001 to Australia
Scott Murray (Saracens), Tom Smith (Brive), Simon Taylor (Edinburgh Reivers)

2005 to New Zealand
Gordon Bulloch (Glasgow Warriors), Chris Cusiter (Border Reivers), Simon Taylor (Edinburgh Rugby), Jason White (Sale Sharks)

— MOTTO SCOTTO —

The order of the thistle was founded by James VII in 1687 and has as its motto "nemo me impune lacessit" ("no-one punishes me with impunity") – hence the decision to have the thistle on the national rugby jersey in every game since 1871.

— FIRST FIVE NATIONS REPLACEMENT —

In 1969, Gordonians scrum-half Ian McCrae was the first player to be used as a replacement in the Five Nations when he went on for Gordon Connell as Scotland beat France 6–3 at Stade Colombes.

— LIONS FALL-OUT —

Much of the rancour between the England and Scotland sides of the 1990s originated from the 1989 Lions tour. In particular, the two sets of forwards had a clash of personalities. When Englishman 'Iron' Mike Teague, who went on to be the player of the tour, dropped a ball in training, his rival for the No.6 spot, John Jeffrey, quipped: "Looks like 'Iron' Mike has got a bit rusty". Only the speedy intervention of several team-mates stopped a training ground ruckus.

— SCOTLAND LEGENDS XV: GREGOR TOWNSEND —

Gregor Townsend: On his day a genius

Borderer Gregor Townsend was first called into the Scotland squad as a 19-year-old and won the last of his 82 caps 11 years later, and still the jury has never managed to return a unanimous verdict. On his day, Scotland's most capped back was a sublime, instinctive genius whose trickery and feints were worth the admission money on their own. But on an off day, Gregor Townsend morphed into the 'Clownsend' caricature that missed touch, ran down blind alleys and threw passes into thin air as he infuriated and disappointed in equal measure.

One of Scotland's few genuinely world-class three-quarters of his generation, Townsend has always claimed that he tried to take on too much because the players around him weren't always capable of doing so, and if you look at the high points of his international career, you can at the very least see his point. Put the mercurial stand-off in top-class company and he was unleashed, unbeatable; place him in the position of No.1 attacking threat and he took on more than even he could deliver.

There were three high watermarks in Townsend's career, and all are unforgettable. The highlight was undoubtedly Townsend's contribution to the 1997 Lions tour to South Africa where, on hard grounds and in the company of the best players in the Home Unions, he looked every inch a world-beater as he broke tackles and made hard yards every time he received the ball.

Not that the inspired 'Toony Flip' which put Gavin Hastings in for the score in 1995 that conjured Scotland's first win in Paris since 1969 comes far behind. Nor, for that matter, does his contribution to Scotland's Championship-winning season in 1999, when he became the first Scot to score a try in every game since the 1925 Grand Slam as Scotland scored 33 first-half points at the Stade de France.

Townsend was always sure of himself and never slow to test himself in the most challenging environment he could find. As a youngster he took himself off to play in Australian club rugby at a time when it could claim to have the best players in the world, and he would later go to play for Heineken Cup champions Northampton before heading to France and finally to Natal Sharks, where he became the only northern hemisphere player to play in the Super 12.

Gregor Townsend vital statistics
Caps: 82 (1993–2003)
Position: Fly-half
Clubs: Gala, Warringah, Northampton, Brive, Castres, Borders, Montpellier, Natal Sharks

— CELEBRITY MARRIAGES —

Kenny Logan, who once had soccer trials as a goalkeeper for Dundee United and Hearts, is married to television sports commentator Gabby Yorath (now Logan, obviously), the daughter of former Wales manager Terry Yorath. Logan's former Scotland team-mate, Melrose No.8 Carl Hogg, is also married to a television personality, commentator Gill Douglas.

— SPRINTING CHAMPS —

Eric Lidell was not the only sprinter of note to play rugby, although he was the only one to play for Scotland. Heriot's and Scotland Schools winger Dougie Walker was the European 200m champion, while Scotland sprinter Elliot Bunney, also a wing with Heriot's (and later Walker's coach and manager), both harboured dreams of playing rugby for Scotland.

— TREMAYNE RODD —

London Scottish scrum-half Tremayne Rodd, who sat on the Conservative benches of the House of Lords as Baron Rennell the Third, won 14 caps for Scotland between 1958–65, playing in the Scotland side which beat Australia 12–8 and the side which drew 0–0 with the All Blacks. He was also a fantastic sevens player and one of the stalwarts of the London Scottish side which won the Middlesex Sevens five times between 1960–65, skills which led to an offer to go to Rugby League.

The nephew of artist Simon Elwes and Nancy Mitford, and a close friend of casino owner John Aspinall and gambler Lord Lucan, Rodd spent nine years in the Navy, during which time he became a Lieutenant and the Navy's boxing champion. His rugby career ended abruptly when he was banned by the IRB for working as a freelance journalist on the disastrous Lions tour to New Zealand in 1966, during which he contributed to *The Observer* and *The Scotsman*.

A larger-than-life character who played rugby for the parliamentary team at the age of 65, he also played cricket, golf, bridge, backgammon and chess for the House of Lords, and was the team leader for Vladimir Kramnik when he beat Garry Kasparov to become World Chess Champion in London in 2000.

— FISHERMAN'S FRIENDS —

Legendary Scotland tighthead prop Iain 'The Bear' Milne is a fanatical fisherman who is part of a group of ex-sportsmen called the Salmon Slayers who regularly fish together. Other members include Welsh rugby legend Gareth Edwards, English cricket's greatest ever all-rounder Ian Botham and former Ireland football manager Jackie Charlton. Their regular haunt is the Whiteadder river in the Borders.

— A WEE DRAM —

The sale of alcohol was banned at football stadia across the country in the aftermath of the 1980 Scottish Cup final between Celtic and Rangers, at which rival Old Firm fans fought on the pitch and police on horseback had to intervene. Murrayfield was excluded from the original draft legislation but the Scottish Rugby Union voluntarily agreed to include Murrayfield in the list of 'dry' stadia, a policy that was only repealed (and then to a limited degree) in 2007.

As a result, pubs such as the *Roseburn* and the *Murrayfield Hotel* have become regular pre-match meeting places for visitors, as have the pubs around Haymarket Station. However, Edinburgh's famous Rose Street – a small road that boasts 16 pubs and which runs between Charlotte Square and St Andrews Square, parallel to George Street and Princes Street – remains the favourite carousing spot for visiting fans. The following are all popular with rugby fans:

The Abbotsford
Rhodes & Co Brasserie and Bar
Milne's Bar
Robertson's 37
The Rose Street Brewery
The Auld Hundred
Brecks
The Fling & Firkin
The Kenilworth
Filthy McNasty's
The Gordon Arms
The Rose and Crown
Olivers
Dirty Dick's
Scott's

— SOCCER CONNECTIONS —

Scotland flanker/wing Roland Reid is the nephew of Rangers forward Don Kitchenbrand. Wing James Craig is the son of Celtic's Jim Craig, one of the Lisbon Lions who won the European Cup in 1967.

— A HALF CENTURY OF CAPS —

At the end of the 2007 Six Nations, Scotland had 21 players who had won 50 or more caps. The youngest player to win 50 caps was Chris Paterson, who reached the landmark in style when he led Scotland out to play South Africa at Murrayfield in November 2004. The oldest player to win 50 caps was tighthead Paul Burnell, who won the 50th of his 52 caps at the ripe old age of 34 in the 1999 World Cup win over Samoa.

The youngest players to reach 50 caps for Scotland are:

Player	Age when awarded 50th cap
Chris Paterson	26
Scott Murray	26
Gregor Townsend	27
Simon Taylor	27
Doddie Weir	27
Jason White	28
Gordon Bulloch	28
Kenny Logan	28
Stuart Grimes	29
Scott Hastings	29
Tony Stander	29
Andy Irvine	31
Jim Renwick	31
Tom Smith	31
Craig Chalmers	31
Bryan Redpath	32
Gary Amstrong	32
Gavin Hastings	33
Colin Deans	33
Sandy Carmichael	33
Paul Burnell	34

— HASTINGS' WORLD CUP RECORD —

As well as being Scotland's leading points scorer of all time, Gavin Hastings is also the leading World Cup points scorer with 227 points to his name from three tournaments. Australia's Michael Lynagh (195), England's Jonny Wilkinson (182) and New Zealand's Grant Fox 170) are next in line.

— SCOTLAND'S GREATEST GAMES 10 —

Scotland 19 England 13
Murrayfield
2nd April 2000

In 1999, it was Scott Gibbs and Wales who thwarted England's Grand Slam plans at the death on the final Sunday of the tournament. In 2000 it was Scotland's Duncan Hodge who inspired a victory so unexpected that the bookmakers were offering 3–1 against Andy Nicol's side before the match.

In many ways the bookies had a point. England had swept all before them until that Sunday while Scotland had shipped 44 points against Ireland, been humiliated in Rome and had merely been well beaten in Cardiff and at home against France. On a freezing cold day where the continual sleet was being swept across Murrayfield by an icy wind, the portents weren't too favourable for coach Ian McGeechan's men.

Nor did it look too handy for much of the first half after England began to apply some early pressure and then registered the first points when Lawrence Dallaglio scuttled over untouched from a five-metre scrum, with Jonny Wilkinson converting and adding a penalty three minutes later.

The turning point came just before half-time when England pounded away at Scotland's line but came away with nothing, due in part to some fearsome hits from debutant blindside Jason White. When Hodge kicked a third penalty just before half-time to bring the Scots back to 10–9 behind, it was game on.

The second half was a brutal, muddy dogfight. One newspaper described it as "Smothering Sunday" as Scotland's tight forwards got up close and personal in their efforts to slow ball and squeeze the life out of an England team determined to run the ball from everywhere on the pitch in total defiance of the Baltic conditions. It was to be their undoing.

With Hodge kicking Scotland into the lead halfway through the second period, the home side began to believe and, with just six minutes remaining, the Scots pack which had gradually got the upper hand on its baffled opponents, drove to deep into the English 22, pushing ever nearer to the English line. When the ball squirted out of yet another ruck, Hodge was on hand to dive over for a try that brought his and Scotland's tally to 19. Despite a stirring late rally from England, the Scots had avoided a first whitewash for 15 years and ruined the start of their visitors' decade as the Welsh had ruined the end of the Nineties for them. With nine of the Scotland team either playing in England or having recently played there a first Calcutta Cup win since 1990 was long overdue and enthusiastically celebrated.

— NUPTIALS INTERRUPTED —

When Alistair Marsh made his wedding plans in 2007, he chose the first free Saturday after the end of the season to make sure that all of his friends and family could be present. May 6th sounded like a plum date: the prop's new side, Edinburgh Accies, had only just been promoted to Division Two and surely wouldn't be troubling the blue riband event of the Scottish club scene, the Cup final, right?

Wrong. When a revitalised Accies side, newly promoted to the top flight, beat much-fancied Boroughmuir in the semi-final of the cup at Raeburn Place, Marsh was forced to fly to Murrayfield from his wedding by a waiting helicopter before rushing back to the reception as soon as hostilities had ceased.

Not that it was a perfect day – Accies were beaten 24–13 by Glasgow Hawks, who themselves had been the first team to win the cup from the Second Division.

— CONSISTENT KICKER —

Chris Paterson kicked a record 19 consecutive successful kicks at goal in the 2007 Six Nations after missing his first kick in the first match of that season against England at Twickenham.

— ALMOST PERFECT —

In an interview, Scotland flanker John Jeffrey described his Kelso farm as "perfect". The interviewer asked him whether there was anything wrong with it at all. "Aye," smiled Jeffrey. "I can see England in the distance."

— PARKER'S ACCOLADE —

Melrose and South of Scotland player Gary Parker, who later became coach of Biggar, Gala and Melrose, had a trial for Hearts Football Club and was twice voted New Zealand football's Most Valuable Player.

— BIG KICK —

In the 1986 Five Nations, Scotland were beaten by Wales only when Paul Thorburn kicked a 70-metre penalty, the longest on record at the time.

— SCOTS IN EXILE —

After the game went professional in 1995, an increasing number of Scottish players tried their luck overseas. The majority went to England, but many others – players such as Gregor Townsend, Bryan Redpath, Tom Smith and Stuart Reid – went to France.

However, with the sacking of Matt Williams after the 2005 Six Nations, and the demise of his much-vaunted 'Fortress Scotland' scheme, where Scotland-based players would be first in line for caps – the trickle of internationals moving from Scotland has become a torrent. By the end of the 2007 World Cup, the following Scottish internationals and Churchill squad members will all be playing their rugby outside of Scotland (with the possibility of them being joined by up to 12 of the internationals at Edinburgh following the fall-out between the SRU and Edinburgh owner Bob Carruthers):

England: Alasdair Dickinson (Gloucester), Lee Dickson (Newcastle Falcons), Ian Fullarton (Saracens), Jim Hamilton (Leicester), Robbie Kydd (Northampton), Rory Lamont (Sale Sharks), Rory Lawson (Gloucester), Sean Lamont (Northampton), Scott Lawson (Sale Sharks), Mark McMillan (Wasps), Euan Murray (Northampton), Chris Paterson (Saracens), Gordon Ross (Saracens), Alasdair Strokosch (Gloucester), Jason White (Sale Sharks)

France: Chris Cusiter (Perpignan), Nathan Hines (Perpignan), Scott Murray (Montauban), Mark Rennie (Bourgoin), Simon Taylor (Stade Francais), Marcus Di Rollo (Toulouse)

Ireland: Rob Dewey (Ulster), Simon Danielli (Ulster)

Wales: Bruce Douglas (Llanelli), Andrew Hall (Dragons), Scott MacLeod (Llanelli), Nikki Walker (Ospreys)

Italy: Barry Irving (Catania)

— SUPER GT —

Gregor Townsend is the only Scot ever to play in the Super 12. He played in seven matches for South Africa's Natal Sharks in 2004 at the age of 31, starting against the Bulls and the Waratahs, and coming off the bench against the Highlanders, Cats, Crusaders, Chiefs and Reds. His solitary try came in the defeat to the Waratahs.

— SCOTLAND LEGENDS XV: HUGH McLEOD —

It is difficult to imagine a Borderer in the 1950s who could get to the ripe old age of 16 before becoming acquainted with the local obsession of rugby, but that's exactly what happened to Hugh McLeod, one of the greatest props ever to come out of Scotland.

However, once McLeod was on first-name terms with the game, there was no stopping him. Less than a year after learning how to play the sport, he was called into the all-conquering Hawick first team as a 17-year-old. Two years later he was representing the South against the touring Springboks and another two years later he was making his Scotland debut against France. By 1959 he was on his second Lions tour, appearing in all six Tests and once memorably taking five heels against the head when playing NZ Universities.

McLeod was one of the most outstanding technicians in front row rugby, but then at 5ft 9in and weighing in at less than 14 stone he had little choice if he was to survive. His secret was an ability to soak up ideas and technical hints like a human sponge, a process that not only enriched him but also made a palpable difference to the game north of the border because few men have added more to the sum of knowledge in Scottish rugby, with the notable exception of Jim Telfer.

The uncompromising McLeod may have been no gentleman once he got onto the pitch, but he was certainly a scholar. Whether it was playing for the South against the Springboks, or bringing back ideas from his Lions tours to South Africa (1955) or Australia and New Zealand (1959), McLeod had an ability to understand what other countries did differently and to filter and communicate the worthwhile lessons. It was this that led directly to Hawick's dominance from the 1950s, but the lessons eventually filtered down to almost every section of Scottish rugby.

McLeod also paid heed himself. He saw the fitness work being done in the southern hemisphere and became a fitness fanatic himself. He also absorbed the technical lessons and became one of the strongest scrummagers in the Five Nations, able to play on either side with equal comfort, and even hooker at a pinch. It was this, allied to a rumbustious nature that loved physical confrontation and a supercharged presence in the loose, that made the astute McLeod such a fearsome opponent.

A down-to-earth Borderer with no airs or graces, Bill McLaren tells a story where McLeod once took lock Frans ten Bos to one side before a match against France and said in his broad brogue: "Frans, I've seen you playing quite a lot and, to be honest I think you're a big lump of potted meat. If I was half your size I'd pick up the nearest Frenchmen and throw him over the bloody stand." The next day the huge lock had a storming game that contributed hugely to Scotland's rare 11–6 win in Paris. "I'd follow that man anywhere," explained Ten Bos.

Hugh McLeod vital statistics
Caps: 40 (1954–62)
Position: Prop
Club: Hawick

— ON THE NET —

Key Scottish rugby websites include:

The SRU site: **www.sru.org.uk** (this is a portal to all club and pro-team websites)
Scottish Rugby online magazine: **www.scrummagazine.com**
Site with streamed TV coverage of games: **www.scottishrugbytv.co**
Site dedicated to coverage of Scottish rugby:
www.scottishrugbyradio.com
Commercial sites: www.planetrugby.com; **www.scrum.com**
For players coming to Scotland: **www.clubworldxv.com**
Forum of Scottish Rugby Supporters: **www.fosrs.org.uk**
Refereeing: **www.edinburgh-refs.co.uk**
Touch rugby: **www.scottishtouch.com**

— CELEBRATORY SONGS —

From the 1999 World Cup, Scotland asked every player to choose a song to be played in the event of that player scoring a try, but quickly abandoned the exercise when it became clear that some of the choices were so obscure that few of the spectators could sing along with them. Instead, they were replaced with two catch-all songs: The Proclaimer's '500 Miles' for tries, and Simple Minds' 'Alive and Kicking' for penalties, conversions and drop goals.

— START OF THE SEVENS —

The game of sevens was invented in the Borders by a butcher in the town of Melrose called Ned Haig. He wasn't actually born in Melrose, originally hailing from Jedburgh, where he was born in December 1858. Haig played for Melrose and even had a couple of games for the south, but the idea that was to make him famous occurred in the early 1880s when the club was in danger of going out of existence due to a lack of funds.

A resourceful soul, Haig put forward the idea of a tournament at which there was athletics and various other sporting pursuits, plus an abbreviated form of rugby with just seven players per side playing games of 15 minutes. He wrote later that: "Want of money made us rack our brains as to what was to be done to keep the club from going to the wall, and the idea struck me that a football tournament might prove attractive but as it was hopeless to think of having several games in one afternoon with 15 players on each side, the teams were reduced to seven men."

So, on 28th April 1883, a crowd of 1,600 thronged in to the Greenyards, with over half that number turning up from Galashiels and a sizeable number from Hawick. The rugby proved to be the star attraction, with a silver cup being presented by The Ladies of Melrose, the forerunner of the famous ladies medals, which are second only to a Scotland cap for Borderers. (In his *Official History of the Melrose Sevens*, Walter Allan recounts an episode in 1983 where several members of the victorious French Barbarians, the first non-British winners of the tournament, handed out their medals to local beauties and caused such offence that they were obliged to scour the town until they found the girls in question so that they could ask for the medals back.)

The destination of the cup turned out to be hotly-contested, with Gala facing hosts Melrose in the final after St Cuthbert's, Selkirk, Gala Forest, St Ronans and Earlston had all been beaten in earlier rounds. Melrose, featuring Ned Haig himself, eventually won in extra-time after a "rough, tough" encounter, but the win wasn't without controversy because as soon as Melrose player Davie Sanderson (also Haig's boss) went over for a try the referee, a Melrose man, declared the home side the winner despite fervent protestations from Gala that there was still plenty of time to play. This is where the 'golden try' precedent comes from.

— ANTHEM POLL —

A poll of Members of the Scottish Parliament by *The Sunday Times* newspaper in 2004 revealed that the majority of MSPs favoured ditching 'Flower of Scotland' as the anthem played before international matches at Murrayfield.

The biggest vote (16 votes) was in favour of commissioning a contemporary composer – such as James MacMillan, royal composer Sir Peter Maxwell-Davies or Travis frontman Fran Healey – while 'Flower of Scotland' (15 votes), 'A Man's a Man' (15) and 'Scots Wha Hae' (12) all attracted strong support from the politicians. 'Freedom Come All Ye' (8), 'God Save the Queen' (8), 'Highland Cathedral' (4), 'Scotland the Brave' (3) and 'Auld Lang Syne' (2) also featured.

Independent MSP Margo MacDonald chose Connie Francis's 'Who's Sorry Now?', Labour MSP Duncan McNeil nominated Patsy Cline's 'Crazy' and Tory MSP Margaret Mitchell suggested 'Ye Cannae Shove Your Granny Aff a Bus'.

— WINNING RUNS —

Scotland's longest winning streak is six matches in a row. This has happened twice: once in 1925/26 when the Grand Slam side beat France, Wales, Ireland, England, France and Wales, and then in 1989/90 when the next Grand Slam side beat Fiji, Romania, Ireland, France, Wales and England in successive matches.

— HEROES TO ZEROES —

The season after Scotland won the Grand Slam in 1984, they were whitewashed and romped away with the Wooden Spoon.

— TRY RECORD —

The biggest number of tries scored in one match by Scotland is 15, which is the number Scotland ran up while thrashing Japan 100–3 at St Johnstone FC's McDiarmid Park ground in Perth in 2004. That match was also the first international in Scotland to have been played north of the Forth.

— DICKINSON AT THE HELM —

Scotland's first coach (his actual title was 'adviser to the captain') was Jordanhill coach Bill Dickinson, who was appointed in 1971 and made an immediate impact. Scotland had lost four of their previous five Championship games, and while they lost the next two matches, the first of those was an unexpectedly close 18–17 loss to a rampant Wales side. The subsequent defeat to Ireland was a disappointment, but Dickinson atoned by coaching his side to two wins over England in the same year – the first a 16–15 Five Nations win at Twickenham courtesy of a last-minute P.C. Brown kick, the second the Centenary celebration match in which John Frame scored a try after 12 seconds and the hosts went on to beat the Auld Enemy 26–6.

When Dickinson was eventually fired from his unpaid post in 1977, he was replaced by outspoken flanker Nairn McEwan, a surprise choice – and not an especially inspired one either as it turned out. Under McEwan, Scotland scorched to the Wooden Spoon before winning just one game in his three seasons in charge.

— TOURING WITH THE LIONS —

Scotland has been very closely associated with leading the Lions down the years. Ian McGeechan and Jim Telfer were both experienced Lions tourists who later coached the world's most famous touring team with conspicuous success.

McGeechan coached the Lions on their successful 1989 tour to Australia and the 1997 tour to South Africa, the only two winning tours since the Lions returned from South Africa in 1974. Telfer accompanied McGeechan to South Africa, where his cameo appearances in the tour video of South Africa, *Living With Lions*, helped make it the most memorable behind-the-scenes rugby documentary ever made.

The legendary Doug Smith, a distinguished former Lion on the 1950 tour of South Africa, also played a part in managing a Lions tour. The former London Scottish player was the manager of the 1971 Lions tour to New Zealand, which was dominated by a mixture of forward power and sublime back play orchestrated by Barry 'The King' John, and which is generally regarded by purists as the apogee of Lions rugby in the modern era.

— SCOTLAND LEGENDS: THE BENCH —

Our 'Scotland Legends XV' would certainly have made an almighty team.

Gavin Hastings; Ian Smith, G.P.S. MacPherson, Gregor Townsend, Andy Irvine; John Rutherford, Gary Armstrong; Ian McLauchlan, Colin Deans, Hugh McLeod, Charles Reid, Gordon Brown, David Bedell-Sivright, Finlay Calder, Mark Morrison.

Here are the impressive replacements who can count themselves unlucky to only have made the bench in this hypothetical dream team:

Doug Elliot (29 caps, 1947–54; flanker with Edinburgh Academicals)
Fast, fearless, abrasive and durable, the 6ft 3in, 14 stone flanker was one of the best breakaways ever to play for Scotland, even if he had the bad luck to play at his country's lowest ebb. A Borders farmer, he was captain when Scotland were pipped 3–0 by the All Blacks in 1953. Elliot was selected for the 1950 Lions tour but couldn't afford to be away from his farm for six months.

Arthur Smith (33 caps, 1955–62; wing with Cambridge University, Gosforth, Ebbw Vale and Edinburgh Wanderers)
A slim winger with incredible changes of direction and pace, Scottish rugby's golden boy was a prolific try-scorer and deadly goalkicker. Smith scored a try on his debut as Scotland broke their 17-match losing streak by beating Wales in the biggest upset of post-war rugby, and never looked back. Capped 33 times without ever being dropped, he skippered both Scotland (including on the 1960 short tour to South Africa) and the British Lions (he toured with them in 1955 and 1962). After obtaining a first in maths he gained a PhD at Cambridge.

David Leslie (32 caps, 1975–85; flanker with Dundee HSFP, West of Scotland and Gala)
Jim Telfer rates David Leslie as the hardest forward he coached and of the Scots only 'Darkie' Bedell-Sivright comes close. However, his fearless play saw Leslie pick up an alarming number of injuries which kept his cap tally artificially low, but when he was fit he was the complete back row forward. Not hugely quick, he intuitively knew where the ball was headed, what decision to take when he got there and had the skills to use the ball to maximum effect. Absolutely crucial to Scotland's 1984 Grand Slam, he was also *Rugby World* magazine's Player of the Year that same year.

Iain Milne (44 caps, 1979–90; tighthead prop with Heriot's FP and Harlequins)

With two small props in our 1st XV, the gargantuan Iain 'The Bear' Milne beats the more mobile Sandy Carmichael to a place on the bench on the basis that he is the best scrummager ever to have played for Scotland. Whether it was in the 1984 Grand Slam game or the 1987 World Cup, Milne (often in tandem with hooker brother Kenny) anchored the scrum while soaking up as much pressure as the opposition could dish out before injuries forced him to quit just before winning a second Grand Slam.

Roy Laidlaw (47 caps, 1980–88; scrum-half with JedForest)

A nuggety little scrum-half in the traditional Borders mould, Laidlaw's searing break kept opposition back rows interested, which in turn gave more space to his perennial halfback partner John Rutherford. An auxiliary flanker when it came to tackling, he was a Grand Slam winner in 1984.

Norman Bruce (31 caps, 1958–64; hooker with Blackheath, the Army and London Scottish)

Had Gala man Norman Bruce not been posted to the Far East by the Army, who knows how many caps he would have won. An unusual hooker for his time, he was fast and generally fairly furious, playing more like a flanker than a front row forward. He scored Scotland's first overseas try when he went on the first short tour to South Africa in 1960.

Wilson Shaw (19 caps, 1934–39; utility back with Glasgow High School FP)

A brilliant runner who could hit full speed off two or three paces, Wilson Shaw's career was hampered by his versatility and the selectors' idiocy, and finally curtailed entirely by the war. A little man who could play fly-half, centre or wing, Shaw was by no means the complete player (*The Scotsman* noted that his tackling was "incredibly slack") but showed what he could do during the 1938 season. Captaining Scotland to a Triple Crown, the last match was at Twickenham where an utterly inspired Shaw scored two tries and made another as Scotland scored five tries to England's one as they won 21–16 in an encounter that immediately became known as 'Wilson Shaw's match'.

— LIONS CAPTAINS —

Scots have been prominent captains of Lions touring parties to have left these shores.

Edinburgh Academical Bill Maclagan was the first Scot to captain the Lions when he took them to South Africa in 1891 on a three-month, 19-match tour that saw the tourists win every match while scoring 221 points and conceding just one. Mark Morrison, who led the Lions to South Africa in 1903 was the next Scottish Lions captain, and the first to return with a series loss after drawing the first two Tests and losing the last. Thanks largely to the presence of some outstanding Welsh three-quarters, Darkie Bedell-Sivright's 1904 side returned from Australia with a record of won 14 lost 0, but in a foretaste of things to come they won only two of their five matches in New Zealand and lost the Test 9–3.

The first post-war Scottish Lions skipper was Edinburgh Wanderers three-quarter Arthur Smith, who led the Lions to South Africa in 1962. Although competitive, his forwards were dominated by their hosts and the party lost three Tests, drawing the fourth. If that record was inauspicious, it was a triumph when compared to the captaincy of Scot Mike Campbell-Lamerton to New Zealand four years later. The veteran second row's side won both Tests in Australia but were whitewashed so comprehensively in the four Tests in New Zealand that Campbell-Lamerton eventually dropped himself.

Arguably the most successful Lions skipper since Maclagan almost exactly a century before, Finlay Calder's captaincy of the Lions to Australia in 1989 proved a triumph with the tourists coming from a Test down to take a gruelling series 2–1 thanks in large part to a David Campese error in the final Test. Gavin Hastings was the seventh Scot to captain the Lions when he led a strong party to New Zealand in 1993, although once again they came a cropper in the land of the long white cloud, winning just one of the four Tests.

— BROTHERS IN ARMS —

The 45 sets of brothers who have played for Scotland are:

- John Arthur (Glasgow Academicals), 2 caps, 1871–72 and Allen Arthur (Glasgow Academicals, 2 caps 1875–76
- William Cross (Merchistonians), 2 caps, 1871–72 and Malcolm Cross (Merchistonians), 9 caps, 1875–80
- James Finlay (Edinburgh Academicals), 4 caps, 1871–75, Arthur Finlay (Edinburgh Academicals), 1 cap, 1875 and Ninian Finlay (Edinburgh Academicals), 9 caps, 1875–81

- Robert Irvine (Edinburgh Academicals), 13 caps, 1871–80 and Duncan Irvine (Edinburgh Academicals), 3 caps, 1878–79
- Thomas Marshall (Edinburgh Academicals), 4 caps, 1871–74 and William Marshall (Edinburgh Academicals), 1 cap, 1872
- J.H. McClure (West of Scotland), 1 cap, 1872 and G.B. McClure (West of Scotland), 1 cap, 1873 +
- James Reid (Edinburgh Wanderers), 5 caps, 1874–77 and Charles Reid (Edinburgh Academicals), 20 caps, 1881–88
- Robert Ainslie (Edinburgh Institution FP), 7 caps, 1879–82 and Thomas Ainslie (Edinburgh Institution FP), 11 caps, 1881–85
- Andrew Don Wauchope (Fettesian-Lorretonians), 12 caps, 1881–88 and Patrick Don Wauchope (Fettesian-Lorretonians), 5 caps, 1885–87
- Robert Maitland (Edinburgh Institution FP), 5 caps, 1881–85 and Gardyne Maitland (Edinburgh Institution FP), 2 caps, 1885
- Archibald Walker (West of Scotland), 5 caps, 1881–83 and James Walker (West of Scotland), 2 caps, 1882–83
- Matthew McEwan (Edinburgh Academicals), 15 caps, 1886–92 and Bill McEwan (Edinburgh Academicals), 16 caps, 1894–1900
- Charles Orr (West of Scotland), 16 caps, 1887–92 and John Orr (West of Scotland), 12 caps, 1889–93
- George Neilson (West of Scotland), 14 caps, 1891–96, Willie Neilson (London Scottish), 14 caps, 1891–97, Gordon Neilson (Merchistonians), 1 cap, 1894 and Robert Neilson (West of Scotland), 6 caps, 1898–1900
- John Dods (Edinburgh Academicals), 8 caps, 1895–97 and Francis Dods (Edinburgh Academicals), 1 cap, 1901
- David Bedell-Sivright (Cambridge University, West of Scotland, Edinburgh University), 22 caps, 1900–08 and John Bedell-Sivright (Cambridge University), 1 cap, 1902
- John Crabbie (Edinburgh Academicals), 6 caps, 1900–05 and George Crabbie (Edinburgh Academicals), 1 cap, 1904
- James Ross (London Scottish), 5 caps, 1901–03 and Edward Ross (London Scottish), 1 cap, 1904
- Lewis MacLeod (Cambridge University), 6 caps, 1904–05 and Ken MacLeod (Cambridge University), 10 caps, 1905–08
- Alex Purves (London Scottish), 10 caps, 1906–08 and William Purves (London Scottish), 6 caps, 1912–13
- Duncan Macgregor (Pontypridd), 3 caps, 1907 and John Macgregor (Edinburgh University), 1 cap, 1909
- Charles Stuart (West of Scotland), 7 caps, 1909–11 and Ludovic Stuart (Glasgow High School FP), 8 caps 1923–30

- Dave Howie (Kirkcaldy), 7 caps, 1912–13 and Bob Howie (Kirkcaldy), 7 caps, 1924–25
- George Murray (Glasgow Academicals), 2 caps, 1921–26 and Ronald Murray (Cambridge University), 2 caps, 1935
- Jimmy Dykes (Glasgow Academicals), 20 caps, 1922–29 and Andrew Dykes (Glasgow Academicals), 1 cap, 1932
- Mac Henderson (Edinburgh Academicals), 3 caps, 1933 and Ian Henderson (Edinburgh Academicals), 8 caps, 1939–48
- Wilson Shaw (Glasgow High School FP), 19 caps, 1934–39 and Ian Shaw (Glasgow High School FP), 1 cap, 1937
- Rab Bruce-Lockhart (London Scottish), 3 caps, 1937–39 and Logie Bruce-Lockhart (London Scottish), 5 caps, 1948–53
- Tom Dorward (Gala), 5 caps, 1938–39 and Arthur Dorward (Gala), 15 caps, 1950–57
- Dave Valentine (Hawick), 2 caps, 1947 and Alec Valentine (RNAS Anthorn), 3 caps, 1953
- Angus Cameron (Glasgow High School FP), 17 caps, 1948–56 and Donald Cameron (Glasgow High School FP), 6 caps, 1953–54
- Robin Chisholm (Melrose), 11 caps, 1955–60 and David Chisholm (Melrose), 14 caps, 1964–68
- Christy Elliot (Langholm), 12 caps, 1958–65 and Tom Elliot (Langholm), 5 caps, 1968–70
- Oliver Grant (Hawick), 6 caps, 1960–64 and Derrick Grant (Hawick), 14 caps, 1965–68
- Cameron Boyle (London Scottish), 3 caps, 1963 and Alasdair Boyle (London Scottish), 6 caps, 1966–68
- Peter Brown (West of Scotland, Gala), 27 caps, 1964–73 and Gordon Brown (West of Scotland), 30 caps, 1969–76
- Brian Gossman (West of Scotland), 3 caps, 1980–83 and Jimmy Gossman (West of Scotland), 1 cap, 1980
- Jim Calder (Stewart's Melville FP), 27 caps, 1981–85 and Finlay Calder (Stewart's Melville FP), 34 caps, 1986–91
- Peter Dods (Gala), 23 caps, 1983–91 and Michael Dods (Gala, Northampton), 8 caps, 1994–96
- Iain Milne (Heriot's FP, Harlequins) 44 caps, 1979–90), Kenny Milne (Heriot's FP), 39 caps, 1989–95 and David Milne (Heriot's FP), 1 cap, 1991
- Gavin Hastings (Watsonians), 61 caps, 1986–95 and Scott Hastings (Watsonians), 65 caps, 1986–97
- John Leslie (Glasgow Caledonians, Sanix, Newcastle, Northampton), 23 caps, 1998–2002 and Martin Leslie (Edinburgh Reivers, Edinburgh Rugby), 37 caps, 1998–2003

- Gordon Bulloch (West of Scotland, Glasgow Caledonians, Glasgow Rugby, 75 caps, 1997–2005 and Alan Bulloch (Glasgow Caledonians), 5 caps, 2000–01, Sean Lamont (Glasgow Rugby, Northampton), 30 caps, (2004–07) and Rory Lamont (Glasgow Rugby), 8 caps, 2005–07

+ It is possible that the McClure's were twins. If so, they would be the first twins to be capped at international level and in Scotland the only other twins to be capped are Jim and Finlay Calder.

In addition, Phipps Turnbull (Edinburgh Academicals), 6 caps, 1901–02 and Gerard Crole (Oxford University), 4 caps, 1920 were half-brothers.

Donald Macdonald (Oxford University, London Scottish, West of Scotland) won 7 caps for Scotland 1977–78 and his older brother Dugald was capped for South Africa against the Lions in 1974.

— LIKE FATHER, LIKE SON —

Fathers and sons who played for Scotland:

- Henry Gedge (London Scottish, Edinburgh Wanderers), 6 caps, 1894–99 and Peter Gedge (Edinburgh Wanderers), 1 cap, 1933
- Joseph Waters (Cambridge University), 2 caps, 1904 and Frank Waters Cambridge University, London Scottish), 7 caps 1930–32
- Irvine Geddes (London Scottish), 6 caps, 1906–08 and Keith Geddes (London Scottish), 4 caps, 1947
- John Bruce-Lockhart (London Scottish), 2 caps, 1913–20 and Rab Bruce-Lockhart (London Scottish), 3 caps, 1937–39 and Logie Bruce-Lockhart (London Scottish), 5 caps, 1948–53
- Allen Sloan (Edinburgh Academicals), 9 caps, 1914–21 and Donald Sloan (Edinburgh Academicals, London Scottish), 7 caps, 1950–53
- Herbert Waddell (Glasgow Academicals), 15 caps, 1924–30 and Gordon Waddell (London Scottish, Devonport Services, Cambridge University), 18 caps, 1957–62
- Max Simmers (Glasgow Academicals), 28 caps, 1926–32 and Brian Simmers (Glasgow Academicals), 7 caps, 1967–71
- Alastair Fisher (Waterloo), 2 caps, 1947 and Colin Fisher (Waterloo), 5 caps, 1975–76
- John Hegarty (Hawick), 6 caps, 1951–55 and Brian Hegarty (Hawick), 4 caps, 1978
- Mike Campbell-Lamerton (Halifax, Army, London Scottish), 23

caps, 1961–66 and Jeremy Campbell-Lamerton (London Scottish), 3 caps, 1986–87
- Ronnie Glasgow (Dunfermline), 10 caps, 1962–65 and Cammie Glasgow (Heriot's FP), 1 cap, 1997
- Sandy Hinshelwood (London Scottish) 21 caps, 1966–70 and Ben Hinshelwood (Worcester), 18 caps, 2002–05
- John Beattie, (Glasgow Academicals), 25 caps, 1980–87 and Johnnie Beattie (Glasgow), 3 caps, 2006–07
- Allan Lawson (Edinburgh Wanderers, London Scottish, Heriot's FP), 15 caps, 1972–80 and Rory Lawson (Gloucester), 6 caps, 2006–07

In addition to those listed, Terry Lineen (Auckland) played in 12 Tests for New Zealand, 1957–60, and his son Sean (Boroughmuir) was capped 29 times for Scotland, 1989–92.

James Craig (West of Scotland, Glasgow Caledonians) who was capped four times for Scotland between 1997–2000, is the son of Jim Craig (Celtic) capped by Scotland at football in 1967.

John and Martin Leslie's (both capped v South Africa in 1998) father Andy was capped by New Zealand in 1974 and led the All Blacks in all ten tests in which he played.

— LIKE GRANDFATHER, LIKE GRANDSON —

Grandfathers and grandsons to play for Scotland:

- George Ritchie (Dundee HSFP), 1 cap, 1932 and Andy Nicol (Dundee HSFP, Bath and Glasgow), 23 caps, 1992–2001

Nicol was also a Lion in 1993, the first British player to lift the Heineken Cup when he led Bath in 1998 and he captained Scotland seven times including the famous Calcutta Cup win at Murrayfield in 2000.

- John Bannerman(Glasgow HSFP), 37 caps, 1921–29 and Shade Munro (Glasgow High/Kelvinside), 7 caps, 1994–97

Bannerman was first capped as a 19-year-old and played in 37 consecutive matches for Scotland, a world record at the time. Munro, also a second row forward, would surely have won many more caps but for a horrendous leg injury. He has made great strides as a coach and is currently assistant to Sean Lineen at Glasgow.

— SCOTLAND'S INTERNATIONAL RESULTS —

SCOTLAND v ENGLAND
Played 124 – Scotland 41, England 66, Drawn 17

1871	Raeburn Place	Scotland 1G 1T to 1T
1872	Kennington Oval	England 1G 1DG 2T to 1DG
1873	Hamilton Crescent	Draw no scoring
1874	Kennington Oval	England 1DG to 1T
1875	Raeburn Place	Draw no scoring
1876	Kennington Oval	England 1G 1T to 0
1877	Raeburn Place	Scotland 1DG to 0
1878	Kennington Oval	Draw no scoring
1879	Raeburn Place	Draw Scotland 1DG England 1G
1880	Whalley Range (Manchester)	England 2G 3T to 1G
1881	Raeburn Place	Draw Scotland 1G 1T England 1DG 1T
1882	Whalley Range (Manchester)	Scotland 2T to 0
1883	Raeburn Place	England 2T to 1T
1884	Blackheath	England 1G to 1T
1886	Raeburn Place	Draw no scoring
1887	Whalley Range (Manchester)	Draw 1T each
1890	Raeburn Place	Scotland 0 England 6
1891	Richmond	England 3 Scotland 9
1892	Raeburn Place	Scotland 0 England 5
1893	Headingley	England 0 Scotland 8
1894	Raeburn Place	Scotland 6 England 0
1895	Richmond	England 3 Scotland 6
1896	Hampden Park	Scotland 11 England 0
1897	Fallowfield (Manchester)	England 8 Scotland 3
1898	Powderhall (Edinburgh)	Scotland 3 England 3
1899	Blackheath	England 0 Scotland 5
1900	Inverleith	Draw no scoring
1901	Blackheath	England 3 Scotland 18
1902	Inverleith	Scotland 3 England 6
1903	Richmond	England 6 Scotland 10
1904	Inverleith	Scotland 6 England 3
1905	Richmond	England 0 Scotland 8
1906	Inverleith	Scotland 3 England 9
1907	Blackheath	England 3 Scotland 8
1908	Inverleith	Scotland 16 England 10
1909	Richmond	England 8 Scotland 18
1910	Inverleith	England 14 Scotland 5
1911	Twickenham	England 13 Scotland 8
1912	Inverleith	Scotland 8 England 3
1913	Twickenham	England 3 Scotland 0
1914	Inverleith	Scotland 15 England 16
1920	Twickenham	England 13 Scotland 4
1921	Inverleith	Scotland 0 England 18
1922	Twickenham	England 11 Scotland 5
1923	Inverleith	Scotland 6 England 8
1924	Twickenham	England 19 Scotland 0
1925	Murrayfield	Scotland 14 England 11
1926	Twickenham	England 9 Scotland 17

1927	Murrayfield	Scotland 21 England 13
1928	Twickenham	England 6 Scotland 0
1929	Murrayfield	Scotland 12 England 6
1930	Twickenham	Draw no scoring
1931	Murrayfield	Scotland 28 England 19
1932	Twickenham	England 16 Scotland 3
1933	Murrayfield	Scotland 3 England 0
1934	Twickenham	England 6 Scotland 3
1935	Murrayfield	Scotland 10 England 7
1936	Twickenham	England 9 Scotland 8
1937	Murrayfield	Scotland 3 England 6
1938	Twickenham	England 16 Scotland 21
1939	Murrayfield	Scotland 6 England 9
1947	Twickenham	England 24 Scotland 5
1948	Murrayfield	Scotland 6 England 3
1949	Twickenham	England 19 Scotland 3
1950	Murrayfield	Scotland 13 England 11
1951	Twickenham	England 5 Scotland 3
1952	Murrayfield	Scotland 3 England 19
1953	Twickenham	England 26 Scotland 8
1954	Murrayfield	Scotland 3 England 13
1955	Twickenham	England 9 Scotland 6
1956	Murrayfield	Scotland 6 England 11
1957	Twickenham	England 16 Scotland 3
1958	Murrayfield	Scotland 3 England 3
1959	Twickenham	England 3 Scotland 3
1960	Murrayfield	Scotland 12 England 21
1961	Twickenham	Scotland 0 England 6
1962	Murrayfield	Scotland 3 England 3
1963	Twickenham	England 10 Scotland 8
1964	Murrayfield	Scotland 15 England 6
1965	Twickenham	England 3 Scotland 3
1966	Murrayfield	Scotland 6 England 3
1967	Twickenham	England 27 England 14
1968	Murrayfield	Scotland 6 England 8
1969	Twickenham	England 8 Scotland 3
1970	Murrayfield	Scotland 14 England 5
1971	Twickenham	England 15 Scotland 16
1971	Murrayfield	Scotland 26 England 6
(Centenary match: non-championship)		
1972	Murrayfield	Scotland 23 England 9
1973	Twickenham	England 20 Scotland 13
1974	Murrayfield	Scotland 16 England 14
1975	Twickenham	England 7 Scotland 6
1976	Murrayfield	Scotland 22 England 12
1977	Twickenham	England 26 Scotland 6
1978	Murrayfield	Scotland 0 England 15
1979	Twickenham	England 7 Scotland 7
1980	Murrayfield	Scotland 18 England 30
1981	Twickenham	England 23 Scotland 17
1982	Murrayfield	Scotland 9 England 9
1983	Twickenham	England 12 Scotland 22
1984	Murrayfield	Scotland 18 England 6
1985	Twickenham	England 10 Scotland 7

1986	Murrayfield	Scotland 33 England 6
1987	Twickenham	England 21 Scotland 12
1988	Murrayfield	Scotland 6 England 9
1989	Twickenham	England 12 Scotland 12
1990	Murrayfield	Scotland 13 England 7
1991	Twickenham	England 21 Scotland 12
1991	Murrayfield (World Cup)	England 9 Scotland 6
1992	Murrayfield	Scotland 7 England 25
1993	Twickenham	England 26 Scotland 12
1994	Murrayfield	Scotland 14 England 15
1995	Twickenham	England 24 Scotland 12
1996	Murrayfield	Scotland 9 England 18
1997	Twickenham	England 41 Scotland 13
1998	Murrayfield	Scotland 20 England 34
1999	Twickenham	England 24 Scotland 21
2000	Murrayfield	Scotland 19 England 13
2001	Twickenham	England 43 Scotland 3
2002	Murrayfield	Scotland 3 England 29
2003	Twickenham	England 40 Scotland 9
2004	Murrayfield	Scotland 13 England 35
2005	Twickenham	England 43 Scotland 22
2006	Murrayfield	Scotland 18 England 12
2007	Twickenham	England 42 Scotland 20

SCOTLAND v WALES
Played 112 – Scotland 48, Wales 61, Drawn 3

1883	Raeburn Place	Scotland 3G to 1G
1884	Newport	Scotland 1DG 1T to 0
1885	Hamilton Crescent	Draw no scoring
1886	Cardiff	Scotland 2G 1T to 0
1887	Raeburn Place	Scotland 4G 8T to 0
1888	Newport	Wales 1T to 0
1889	Raeburn Place	Scotland 2T to 0
1890	Cardiff	Wales 2 Scotland 8
1891	Raeburn Place	Scotland 15 Wales 0
1892	Swansea	Wales 3 Scotland 7
1893	Raeburn Place	Scotland 0 Wales 9
1894	Newport	Wales 7 Scotland 0
1895	Raeburn Place	Scotland 5 Wales 4
1896	Cardiff	Scotland 0 Wales 6
1899	Inverleith	Scotland 21 Wales 10
1900	Swansea	Wales 12 Scotland 3
1901	Inverleith	Wales 8 Scotland 18
1902	Cardiff	Wales 14 Scotland 5
1903	Inverleith	Scotland 6 Wales 0
1904	Swansea	Wales 21 Wales 3
1905	Inverleith	Scotland 3 Wales 6
1906	Cardiff	Wales 9 Scotland 3
1907	Inverleith	Scotland 6 Wales 3
1908	Swansea	Wales 6 Scotland 5
1909	Inverleith	Scotland 3 Wales 5
1910	Cardiff	Wales 14 Scotland 0
1911	Inverleith	Scotland 10 Wales 32
1912	Swansea	Wales 21 Scotland 6
1913	Inverleith	Scotland 0 Wales 8

1914	Cardiff	Wales 24 Scotland 5
1920	Inverleith	Scotland 9 Wales 5
1921	Swansea	Wales 8 Scotland 14
1922	Inverleith	Draw Scotland 9 Wales 9
1923	Cardiff	Wales 8 Scotland 11
1924	Inverleith	Scotland 35 Wales 10
1925	Swansea	Wales 14 Scotland 24
1926	Murrayfield	Scotland 8 Wales 5
1927	Cardiff	Wales 0 Scotland 5
1928	Murrayfield	Scotland 0 Wales 13
1929	Swansea	Wales 14 Scotland 7
1930	Murrayfield	Scotland 12 Wales 9
1931	Cardiff	Wales 13 Scotland 8
1932	Murrayfield	Scotland 0 Wales 6
1933	Swansea	Wales 3 Scotland 11
1934	Murrayfield	Scotland 6 Wales 13
1935	Cardiff	Wales 10 Scotland 6
1936	Murrayfield	Scotland 3 Wales 13
1937	Swansea	Wales 6 Scotland 13
1938	Murrayfield	Scotland 8 Wales 6
1939	Cardiff	Wales 11 Scotland 3
1947	Murrayfield	Scotland 8 Wales 22
1948	Cardiff	Wales 14 Scotland 0
1949	Murrayfield	Scotland 6 Wales 5
1950	Swansea	Wales 12 Scotland 0
1951	Murrayfield	Scotland 19 Wales 0
1952	Cardiff	Wales 11 Scotland 0
1953	Murrayfield	Scotland 0 Wales 12
1954	Swansea	Wales 15 Scotland 3
1955	Murrayfield	Scotland 14 Wales 8
1956	Cardiff	Wales 9 Scotland 3
1957	Murrayfield	Scotland 9 Wales 6
1958	Cardiff	Wales 8 Scotland 3
1959	Murrayfield	Scotland 6 Wales 5
1960	Cardiff	Wales 8 Scotland 0
1961	Murrayfield	Scotland 3 Wales 0
1962	Cardiff	Wales 3 Scotland 8
1963	Murrayfield	Scotland 0 Wales 6
1964	Cardiff	Wales 11 Scotland 3
1965	Murrayfield	Scotland 12 Wales 14
1966	Cardiff	Wales 8 Scotland 3
1967	Murrayfield	Scotland 11 Wales 5
1968	Cardiff	Wales 5 Scotland 0
1969	Murrayfield	Scotland 3 Wales 17
1970	Cardiff	Wales 18 Scotland 9
1971	Murrayfield	Scotland 18 Wales 19
1972	Cardiff	Wales 35 Scotland 12
1973	Murrayfield	Scotland 10 Wales 9
1974	Cardiff	Wales 6 Scotland 0
1975	Murrayfield	Scotland 12 Wales 10
1976	Cardiff	Wales 28 Scotland 6
1977	Murrayfield	Wales Scotland 9 Wales 18
1978	Cardiff	Wales 22 Scotland 14
1979	Murrayfield	Scotland 13 Wales 19
1980	Cardiff	Wales 17 Scotland 6

1981	Murrayfield	Scotland 15 Wales 6
1982	Cardiff	Wales 18 Scotland 34
1983	Murrayfield	Scotland 15 Wales 19
1984	Cardiff	Wales 9 Scotland 15
1985	Murrayfield	Scotland 21 Wales 25
1986	Cardiff	Wales 22 Scotland 15
1987	Murrayfield	Scotland 21 Wales 15)
1988	Cardiff	Wales 25 Scotland 20
1989	Murrayfield	Scotland 23 Wales 7
1990	Cardiff	Wales 9 Scotland 13
1991	Murrayfield	Scotland 32 Wales 12
1992	Cardiff	Wales 15 Scotland 9
1993	Murrayfield	Scotland 20 Wales 0
1994	Cardiff	Wales 1G 4PG 2T (29) to 2PG (6)
1995	Murrayfield	Scotland 26 Wales 13
1996	Cardiff	Wales 14 Scotland 16
1997	Murrayfield	Scotland 19 Wales 34
1998	Wembley	Wales 19 Scotland 13
1999	Murrayfield	Scotland 33 Wales 20
2000	Cardiff (Millennium Stadium)	Wales 26 Scotland 18
2001	Murrayfield	Draw Scotland 28 Wales 28
2002	Cardiff (Millennium Stadium)	Wales 22 Scotland 27
2003	Murrayfield	Scotland 30 Wales 22
2003	Cardiff (Millennium Stadium) (non-championship)	Wales 23 Scotland 9
2004	Cardiff (Millennium Stadium)	Wales 23 Scotland 10
2005	Murrayfield	Scotland 22 Wales 46
2006	Cardiff (Millennium Stadium)	Wales 28 Scotland 18
2007	Murrayfield	Scotland 21 Wales 9

SCOTLAND v IRELAND
Played 120 – Scotland 61, Ireland 53, Drawn 5, Abandoned 1

1877	Ormeau (Belfast)	Scotland 4G 2DG 2T to 0
1879	Ormeau (Belfast)	Scotland 1G 1DG 1T to 0
1880	Hamilton Crescent	Scotland 1G 2DG 2T to 0
1881	Ormeau (Belfast)	Ireland 1DG to 1T
1882	Hamilton Crescent	Ireland 2T to 0
1883	Ormeau (Belfast)	Scotland 1G 1T to 0
1884	Raeburn Place	Scotland 2G 2T to 1T
1885	Ormeau (Belfast)	Abandoned Scotland 1T Ireland 0
1885	Raeburn Place	Scotland 1G 2T to 0
1886	Raeburn Place	Scotland 3G 1DG 2T to 0
1887	Ormeau (Belfast)	Scotland 1G 1GM 2T to 0
1888	Raeburn Place	Scotland 1G to 0
1889	Ormeau (Belfast)	Scotland 1DG to 0
1890	Raeburn Place	Scotland 5 Ireland 0
1891	Ballynafeigh (Belfast)	Ireland 0 Scotland 14
1892	Raeburn Place	Scotland 2 Ireland 0
1893	Ballynafeigh (Belfast)	Ireland 0 Scotland 0
1894	Lansdowne Road	Ireland 5 Scotland 0
1895	Raeburn Place	Scotland 6 Ireland 0
1896	Lansdowne Road	Ireland 0 Scotland 0
1897	Powderhall (Edinburgh)	Scotland 8 Ireland 3
1898	Balmoral (Belfast)	Ireland 0 Scotland 8
1899	Inverleith	Scotland 3 Ireland 9

1900	Lansdowne Road	Ireland 0 Scotland 0
1901	Inverleith	Scotland 9 Ireland 5
1902	Balmoral (Belfast)	Ireland 5 Scotland 0
1903	Inverleith	Scotland 3 Ireland 0
1904	Lansdowne Road	Ireland 3 Scotland 19
1905	Inverleith	Scotland 5 Ireland 11
1906	Lansdowne Road	Ireland 6 Scotland 13
1907	Inverleith	Scotland 15 Ireland 3
1908	Lansdowne Road	Ireland 16 Scotland 11
1909	Inverleith	Scotland 9 Ireland 3
1910	Balmoral (Belfast)	Ireland 0 Scotland 14
1911	Inverleith	Scotland 10 Ireland 16
1912	Lansdowne Road	Ireland 10 Scotland 8
1913	Inverleith	Scotland 29 Ireland 14
1914	Lansdowne Road	Ireland 6 Scotland 0
1920	Inverleith	Scotland 19 Ireland 0
1921	Lansdowne Road	Ireland 9 Scotland 8
1922	Inverleith	Scotland 6 Ireland 3
1923	Lansdowne Road	Ireland 3 Scotland 13
1924	Inverleith	Scotland 13 Ireland 8
1925	Lansdowne Road	Ireland 8 Scotland 14
1926	Murrayfield	Scotland 0 Ireland 3
1927	Lansdowne Road	Ireland 6 Scotland 0
1928	Murrayfield	Scotland 5 Ireland 13
1929	Lansdowne Road	Ireland 7 Scotland 16
1930	Murrayfield	Scotland 11 Ireland 14
1931	Lansdowne Road	Ireland 8 Scotland 5
1932	Murrayfield	Scotland 8 Ireland 20
1933	Lansdowne Road	Ireland 6 Scotland 8
1934	Murrayfield	Scotland 16 Ireland 9
1935	Lansdowne Road	Ireland 12 Scotland 5
1936	Murrayfield	Scotland 4 Ireland 10
1937	Lansdowne Road	Ireland 11 Scotland 4
1938	Murrayfield	Scotland 23 Ireland 14
1939	Lansdowne Road	Ireland 12 Scotland 3
1947	Murrayfield	Scotland 0 Ireland 3
1948	Lansdowne Road	Ireland 6 Scotland 0
1949	Murrayfield	Scotland 3 Ireland 13
1950	Lansdowne Road	Ireland 21 Scotland 0
1951	Murrayfield	Scotland 5 Ireland 6
1952	Lansdowne Road	Ireland 12 Scotland 8
1953	Murrayfield	Scotland 8 Ireland 26
1954	Ravenhill (Belfast)	Ireland 6 Scotland 0
1955	Murrayfield	Scotland 12 Ireland 3
1956	Lansdowne Road	Ireland 14 Scotland 10
1957	Murrayfield	Scotland 3 Ireland 5
1958	Lansdowne Road	Ireland 12 Scotland 6
1959	Murrayfield	Scotland 3 Ireland 8
1960	Lansdowne Road	Ireland 5 Scotland 6
1961	Murrayfield	Scotland 16 Ireland 8
1962	Lansdowne Road	Ireland 6 Scotland 20
1963	Murrayfield	Scotland 3 Ireland 0
1964	Lansdowne Road	Ireland 3 Scotland 6
1965	Murrayfield	Scotland 3 Ireland 16
1966	Lansdowne Road	Ireland 3 Scotland 11

1967	Murrayfield	Scotland 3 Ireland 5
1968	Lansdowne Road	Ireland 14 Scotland 6
1969	Murrayfield	Scotland 0 Ireland 16
1970	Lansdowne Road	Ireland 16 Scotland 11
1971	Murrayfield	Scotland 5 Ireland 17
1972	No Match	
1973	Murrayfield	Scotland 19 Ireland 14
1974	Lansdowne Road	Ireland 9 Scotland 6
1975	Murrayfield	Scotland 20 Ireland 13
1976	Lansdowne Road	Ireland 6 Scotland 15
1977	Murrayfield	Scotland 21 Ireland 18
1978	Lansdowne Road	Ireland 12 Scotland 9
1979	Murrayfield	Scotland 11 Ireland 11
1980	Lansdowne Road	Ireland 22 Scotland 15
1981	Murrayfield	Scotland 10 Ireland 9
1982	Lansdowne Road	Ireland 21 Scotland 12
1983	Murrayfield	Ireland 15 Scotland 13
1984	Lansdowne Road	Ireland 9 Scotland 32
1985	Murrayfield	Scotland 15 Ireland 18
1986	Lansdowne Road	Ireland 9 Scotland 10
1987	Murrayfield	Scotland 16 Ireland 12
1988	Lansdowne Road	Ireland 22 Scotland 18
1989	Murrayfield	Scotland 37 Ireland 21
1990	Lansdowne Road	Ireland 10 Scotland 13
1991	Murrayfield	Scotland 28 Ireland 25
1991	Murrayfield (World Cup)	Scotland 24 Ireland 15
1992	Lansdowne Road	Ireland 10 Scotland 18
1993	Murrayfield	Scotland 15 Ireland 3
1994	Lansdowne Road	Ireland 6 Scotland 6
1995	Murrayfield	Scotland 26 Ireland 13
1996	Lansdowne Road	Ireland 10 Scotland 16
1997	Murrayfield	Scotland 38 Ireland 10
1998	Lansdowne Road	Ireland 16 Scotland 17
1999	Murrayfield	Scotland 30 Ireland 13
2000	Lansdowne Road	Ireland 44 Scotland 22
2001	Murrayfield	Scotland 32 Ireland 10
2002	Lansdowne Road	Ireland 43 Scotland 22
2003	Murrayfield	Scotland 6 Ireland 36
2003	Murrayfield (non-championship)	Scotland 10 Ireland 29
2004	Lansdowne Road	Ireland 37 Scotland 16
2005	Murrayfield	Scotland 13 Ireland 40
2006	Lansdowne Road	Ireland 15 Scotland 9
2007	Murrayfield	Scotland 18 Ireland 19

SCOTLAND v FRANCE
Played 80 – Scotland 34, France 43, Drawn 3

1910	Inverleith	Scotland 27 France 0
1911	Colombes	France 16 Scotland 15
1912	Inverleith	Scotland 31 France 3
1913	Parc des Princes	France 3 Scotland 21
1920	Parc des Princes	France 0 Scotland 5
1921	Inverleith	Scotland 0 France 3
1922	Colombes	France 3 Scotland 3
1923	Inverleith	Scotland 16 France 3
1924	Stade Pershing	France 12 Scotland 10

1925	Inverleith	Scotland 25 France 4
1926	Colombes	France 6 Scotland 20
1927	Murrayfield	Scotland 23 France 6
1928	Colombes	France 6 Scotland 15
1929	Murrayfield	Scotland 6 France 3
1930	Colombes	France 7 Scotland 3
1931	Murrayfield	Scotland 6 France 4
1947	Colombes	France 8 Scotland 3
1948	Murrayfield	Scotland 9 France 8
1949	Colombes	France 0 Scotland 8
1950	Murrayfield	Scotland 8 France 5
1951	Colombes	France 14 Scotland 12
1952	Murrayfield	Scotland 11 France 13
1953	Colombes	France 11 Scotland 5
1954	Murrayfield	Scotland 0 France 3
1955	Colombes	France 15 Scotland 0
1956	Murrayfield	Scotland 12 Scotland 0
1957	Colombes	France 0 Scotland 6
1958	Murrayfield	Scotland 11 France 9
1959	Colombes	France 9 Scotland 0
1960	Murrayfield	Scotland 11 France 13
1961	Colombes	France 11 Scotland 0
1962	Murrayfield	Scotland 3 France 11
1963	Colombes	France 6 Scotland 11
1964	Murrayfield	Scotland 10 France 0
1965	Colombes	France 16 Scotland 8
1966	Murrayfield	Scotland 3 France 3
1967	Colombes	France 8 Scotland 9
1968	Murrayfield	Scotland 6 France 8
1969	Colombes	France 3 Scotland 6
1970	Murrayfield	Scotland 9 France 11
1971	Colombes	France 13 Scotland 8
1972	Murrayfield	Scotland 20 France 9
1973	Parc des Princes	France 16 Scotland 13
1974	Murrayfield	Scotland 19 France 6
1975	Parc des Princes	France 10 Scotland 9
1976	Murrayfield	Scotland 6 France 13
1977	Parc des Princes	France 23 Scotland 3
1978	Murrayfield	Scotland 16 France 19
1979	Parc des Princes	France 21 Scotland 17
1980	Murrayfield	Scotland 22 France 14
1981	Parc des Princes	France 16 Scotland 9
1982	Murrayfield	Scotland 16 France 7
1983	Parc des Princes	France 19 Scotland 15
1984	Murrayfield	Scotland 21 France 12
1985	Parc des Princes	France 11 Scotland 3
1986	Murrayfield	Scotland 18 Scotland 17
1987	Parc des Princes	France 28 Scotland 22
1987	Christchurch (World Cup)	Scotland 20 France 20
1988	Murrayfield	Scotland 23 France 12
1989	Parc des Princes	France 19 Scotland 3
1990	Murrayfield	Scotland 21 France 0
1991	Parc des Princes	France 15 Scotland 9
1992	Murrayfield	Scotland 10 France 6
1993	Parc des Princes	France 14 Scotland 3

1994	Murrayfield	Scotland 12 France 20
1995	Parc des Princes	France 21 Scotland 23
1995	Pretoria (World Cup)	France 22 Scotland 19
1996	Murrayfield	Scotland 19 France 14
1997	Parc des Princes	France 47 Scotland 20
1998	Murrayfield	Scotland 16 France 51
1999	Stade de France	France 22 Scotland 36
2000	Murrayfield	Scotland 16 France 28
2001	Stade de France	France 16 Scotland 6
2002	Murrayfield	Scotland 10 France 22
2003	Stade de France	France 38 Scotland 3
2003	Sydney (Telstra Stadium) (World Cup)	France 51 Scotland 9
2004	Murrayfield	Scotland 0 France 31
2005	Stade de France	France 16 Scotland 9
2006	Murrayfield	Scotland 20 France 16
2007	Stade de France	France 46 Scotland 19

SCOTLAND v ITALY
Played 12 – Scotland 8, Italy 4

1996	Murrayfield	Scotland 29 Italy 22
1998	Stadio di Monigo (Treviso)	Italy 25 Scotland 21
1999	Murrayfield	Scotland 30 Italy 12
2000	Stadio Flaminio (Rome)	Italy 34 Scotland 20
2001	Murrayfield	Scotland 23 Italy 19
2002	Stadio Flaminio (Rome)	Italy 12 Scotland 29
2003	Murrayfield	Scotland 33 Italy 25
2003	Murrayfield (non-championship)	Scotland 47 Italy 15
2004	Stadio Flaminio (Rome)	Italy 20 Scotland 14
2005	Murrayfield	Scotland 18 Italy 10
2006	Stadio Flaminio (Rome)	Italy 10 Scotland 13
2007	Murrayfield	Scotland 17 Italy 37

(Italy joined the Six Nations' Championship in 2000)

SCOTLAND v NEW ZEALAND
Played 25 – New Zealand 23, Drawn 2

1905	Inverleith	Scotland 7 New Zealand 12
1935	Murrayfield	Scotland 8 New Zealand 18
1954	Murrayfield	Scotland 0 New Zealand 3
1964	Murrayfield	Scotland 0 New Zealand 0
1967	Murrayfield	Scotland 3 New Zealand 14
1972	Murrayfield	Scotland 9 New Zealand 14
1975	Auckland	New Zealand 24 Scotland 0
1978	Murrayfield	Scotland 9 New Zealand 18
1979	Murrayfield	Scotland 6 New Zealand 20
1981	Dunedin	New Zealand 11 Scotland 4
1981	Auckland	New Zealand 40 Scotland 15
1983	Murrayfield	Scotland 25 New Zealand 25
1987	Christchurch (World Cup)	New Zealand 30 Scotland 3
1990	Dunedin	New Zealand 31 Scotland 16
1990	Auckland	New Zealand 21 Scotland 18
1991	Cardiff (World Cup)	New Zealand 13 Scotland 6
1993	Murrayfield	Scotland 15 New Zealand 51
1995	Pretoria (World Cup)	New Zealand 48 Scotland 30
1996	Dunedin	New Zealand 62 Scotland 31

1996	Auckland	New Zealand 36 Scotland 12
1999	Murrayfield (World Cup)	Scotland 18 New Zealand 30
2000	Dunedin	New Zealand 69 Scotland 20
2000	Auckland	New Zealand 48 Scotland 14
2001	Murrayfield	Scotland 6 New Zealand 37
2005	Murrayfield	Scotland 10 New Zealand 29

SCOTLAND v SOUTH AFRICA
Played 19 – Scotland 4, South Africa 15

1906	Hampden Park	Scotland 6 South Africa 0
1912	Inverleith	Scotland 0 South Africa 16
1932	Murrayfield	Scotland 3 South Africa 6
1951	Murrayfield	Scotland 0 South Africa 44
1960	Port Elizabeth	South Africa 18 Scotland 10
1961	Murrayfield	Scotland 5 South Africa 12
1965	Murrayfield	Scotland 8 South Africa 5
1969	Murrayfield	Scotland 6 South Africa 3
1994	Murrayfield	Scotland 10 South Africa 34
1997	Murrayfield	Scotland 10 South Africa 68
1998	Murrayfield	Scotland 10 South Africa 35
1999	Murrayfield (World Cup)	South Africa 46 Scotland 29
2002	Murrayfield	Scotland 21 South Africa 6
2003	Durban	South Africa 29 Scotland 25
2003	Johannesburg	South Africa 28 Scotland 19
2004	Murrayfield	Scotland 10 South Africa 45
2006	Durban	South Africa 36 Scotland 16
2006	Port Elizabeth	South Africa 29 Scotland 15
2007	Murrayfield	Scotland 3 South Africa 27

SCOTLAND v NEW SOUTH WALES

| 1927 | Murrayfield | Scotland 10 NSW 8 |

SCOTLAND v AUSTRALIA
Played 23 – Scotland 6, Australia 17

1947	Murrayfield	Scotland 7 Australia 16
1958	Murrayfield	Scotland 12 Australia 8
1966	Murrayfield	Scotland 11 Australia 5
1968	Murrayfield	Scotland 9 Australia 3
1970	Sydney Cricket Ground	Australia 23 Scotland 3
1975	Murrayfield	Scotland 10 Australia 3
1981	Murrayfield	Scotland 24 Australia 15
1982	Ballymore (Brisbane)	Australia 7 Scotland 12
1982	Sydney Cricket Ground	Australia 33 Scotland 9
1984	Murrayfield	Scotland 12 Australia 37
1988	Murrayfield	Scotland 13 Australia 32
1992	Sydney Football Stadium	Australia 27 Scotland 12
1992	Ballymore (Brisbane)	Australia 37 Scotland 13
1996	Murrayfield	Scotland 19 Australia 29
1997	Murrayfield	Scotland 8 Australia 37
1998	Sydney Football Stadium	Australia 45 Scotland 3
1998	Ballymore (Brisbane)	Australia 33 Scotland 11
2000	Murrayfield	Scotland 9 Australia 30
2003	Brisbane (Suncorp Stadium) (World Cup)	Australia 33 Scotland 16
2004	Melbourne (Telstra Dome)	Australia 35 Scotland 15

2004	Sydney (Telstra Stadium)	Australia 34 Scotland 3
2004	Murrayfield	Scotland 14 Australia 31
2004	Hampden Park	Scotland 17 Australia 31

SCOTLAND v ARGENTINA
Played 6 – Scotland 1, Argentina 5

1969	Buenos Aires (not full international)	Argentina 20 Scotland XV 3
1969	Buenos Aires (not full international)	Argentina 3 Scotland XV 6
1973	Murrayfield (not full international)	Scotland XV 12 Argentina 11
1990	Murrayfield	Scotland 49 Argentina 3
1994	Buenos Aires	Argentina 16 Scotland 15
1994	Buenos Aires	Argentina 19 Scotland 17
1999	Murrayfield	Scotland 22 Argentina 31
2001	Murrayfield	Scotland 16 Argentina 25
2005	Murrayfield	Scotland 19 Argentina 23

(The countries have met on three other occasions when Scotland did not award caps)

SCOTLAND v CANADA

1991	Saint John, New Brunswick (not full international)	Canada 24 Scotland 19
1995	Murrayfield	Scotland 22 Canada 6
2002	Vancouver (Thunderbird Stadium)	Canada 26 Scotland 23

SCOTLAND v FIJI

1989	Murrayfield	Scotland 38 Fiji 17
1998	Suva	Fiji 51 Scotland 26
2002	Murrayfield	Scotland 36 Fiji 22
2003	Sydney (Aussie Stadium) (World Cup)	Scotland 22 Fiji 20

(The countries met also in 1982 and 1993, but Scotland did not award caps)

SCOTLAND v IVORY COAST

| 1995 | Rustenberg (World Cup) | Scotland 89 Ivory Coast 0 |

SCOTLAND v JAPAN

1991	Murrayfield (World Cup)	Scotland 47 Japan 9
2003	Townsville (World Cup)	Scotland 32 Japan 11
2004	Perth (McDiarmid Park)	Scotland 100 Japan 8

(The countries have met on four other occasions when Scotland did not award caps)

SCOTLAND v ROMANIA
Played 11 – Scotland 9, Romania 2

1981	Murrayfield	Scotland 12 Romania 6
1984	Bucharest	Romania 28 Scotland 22
1986	Bucharest	Romania 18 Scotland 33
1987	Dunedin (World Cup)	Scotland 55 Romania 28
1989	Murrayfield	Scotland 32 Romania 0
1991	Bucharest	Romania 18 Scotland 12
1995	Murrayfield	Scotland 49 Romania 16
1999	Hampden Park	Scotland 60 Romania 19
2002	Murrayfield	Scotland 37 Romania 10
2005	Bucharest	Scotland 39 Romania 19
2007	Murrayfield	Scotland 46 Romania 6

SCOTLAND v SAMOA *(formerly Western Samoa)*
Played 6 – Scotland 5, drawn 1

1991	Murrayfield (World Cup)	Scotland 28 Western Samoa 6
1995	Murrayfield	Scotland 15 Western Samoa 15
1999	Murrayfield (World Cup)	Scotland 35 Samoa 20
2000	Murrayfield	Scotland 31 Samoa 8
2004	Wellington, New Zealand (Westpac Stadium)	Scotland 38 Samoa 3
2005	Murrayfield	Scotland 18 Samoa 11

(The countries met in 1993, but Scotland did not award caps)
(Samoa changed name from Western Samoa in 1997)

SCOTLAND v PACIFIC ISLANDERS *(Fiji, Samoa and Tonga)*
2007   Murrayfield   Scotland 34 Pacific Islanders 22

SCOTLAND v SPAIN
1999   Murrayfield (World Cup)   Scotland 48 Spain 0
(The countries have met on four other occasions when Scotland did not award caps)

SCOTLAND v TONGA
1995   Pretoria (World Cup)   Scotland 41 Tonga 5
2001   Murrayfield   Scotland 43 Tonga 20
(The countries met also in 1974 and 1993, but Scotland did not award caps)

SCOTLAND v URUGUAY
1999   Murrayfield (World Cup)   Scotland 43 Uruguay 12

SCOTLAND v USA
2000   Murrayfield   Scotland 53 USA 6
2002   San Francisco (Balboa Park)   USA 23 Scotland 65
2003   Brisbane (Suncorp Stadium)   Scotland 39 USA 15
        (World Cup)
(The countries also met in 1991, when Scotland did not award caps)

SCOTLAND v ZIMBABWE
1987   Wellington (Athletic Park)   Scotland 60 Zimbabwe 21
        (World Cup)
1991   Murrayfield (World Cup)   Scotland 51 Zimbabwe 12
(The countries met on five other occasions when Scotland did not award caps)

SCOTLAND v SRU PRESIDENT'S XV
1973   Murrayfield   Scotland 27 President's XV 16

1946 VICTORY INTERNATIONALS

Scotland 11	New Zealand Army 6	(Murrayfield)
Wales 6	Scotland 25	(Swansea)
Scotland 9	Ireland 0	(Murrayfield)
England 12	Scotland 8	(Twickenham)
Scotland 13	Wales 11	(Murrayfield)
Scotland 27	England 0	(Murrayfield)